Warriors in Life

Facing and Overcoming our Challenges

Delisa Lindsey

Copyright © 2014 Delisa Lindsey

All rights reserved.

ISBN-13: 978-1499553451

ISBN-10: 1499553455

Unless otherwise stated, all Scripture Quotations taken from the King James Version of the Holy Bible. All Rights Reserved.

Published by
It's All About Him Media & Publishing
A Multimedia Division of True Love Church of Refuge
5201-D Nations Ford Road
Charlotte, NC 28217
www.truelovechurchofrefuge.org
www.aahmp.weebly.com
www.facebook.com/ItsAllAboutHimMediaPublishing
980-522-8096

Chief Editor and Cover Design
Delisa Lindsey

Printed in the United States of America. All rights reserved under International Copyright Law Contents and/or cover may not be reproduced in whole or in part without express written consent of the publisher.

Warriors in Life

DEDICATION

I dedicate this book to every believer who is steadfast in the faith. Life has challenges, in fact it is filled with challenges but through the grace of God we can all overcome it. Let this book encourage and inspire you to search deep within yourself, see you for who you really are, and embrace the journey to becoming a stronger, better you. You are a warrior in life and the half has yet to be told.

CONTENTS

	Acknowledgments	i
1	Overcoming Childhood Traumas	1
2	Overcoming Sexual Abuse	Pg 15
3	Overcoming the Love of Money	Pg 25
4	WWJD?	Pg 31
5	Overcoming the Beast of Debt	Pg 37
6	Overcoming Stinginess	Pg 51
7	Overcoming the Identity Crisis	Pg 59
8	Overcoming with Church Leadership	Pg 65
9	Overcoming Messiness in Ministry	Pg 71
10	Overcoming While Living with Unbelievers	Pg 75
11	Overcoming As A Minister	Pg 79
12	Overcoming with Unbelieving Spouses/Family	Pg 87
13	Overcoming in Physical Health	Pg 103
14	Overcoming in Emotional Health	Pg 111
15	Warriors in Life – Author's Summary	Pg 123

ACKNOWLEDGMENTS

Father, You are my inspiration. I live for You and breathe for You. You are the source of my everything.

To my husband, Apostle John Lindsey, I love you with all of my heart. You are indeed a Warrior in life.

To my church family, my spiritual sons and daughters at True Love Church of Refuge in Charlotte, NC, you guys rock!!! You are all indeed Warriors in life.

And to every man and woman of God who is holding up the Blood Stained Banner of the Lord, Jesus Christ, you are Warriors in Life…

TWO FORMER STUDENT FROM THE SCHOOL OF WARRIORS (FROM WHICH THIS BOOK IS WRITTEN) WRITES:

I thoroughly enjoyed the course - "School of Warriors" – I would say it was a warfare teaching on the "inner me"! To be an effective minister; carrier of the gospel we must confront specific areas in our lives that could hinder our effectiveness. I love how Father orchestrated each course – Warriors in Life, Finance, Ministry, Family, Physical and Emotional Health and it is imperative that we are healed in all of these areas. I loved the intimacy of the class where we were free to share and the atmosphere conducive for God to move. I learned so much about myself and as a result of this class I am excited about what's next for me in my kingdom assignment as I apply what I've learned to my life. 1 Timothy 3:2-7 outlines characteristics of godly leadership and the School of Warriors was preparation to develop and understand those characteristics. I look forward to the next school offered by True Love Apostolic College. God bless you for all that you pour out!
– Evang. Marva Roseborough

The School of Warriors taught by Prophetess Delisa Lindsey is nothing short of life changing! When you begin the course it begins at the very heart and core of who we are as individuals of the kingdom...it starts with YOU. It focuses on the various dimensions that formulate who we are and how we function in life in the areas of identity, finances, ministry and family. While the studies in themselves are complex in nature they are very simplified to where all walks of life are able to grasp the knowledge of it and soar. Prophetess Lindsey's course far exceeded my expectations and I am so glad to have been blessed with an opportunity to experience the teaching. I recommend any and everyone who is kingdom minded

and maybe struggling with ministry and your assignment to take the school of Warriors, you will never regret it.
- Veronica E. Patterson

Delisa Lindsey

1

OVERCOMING OUR CHILDHOOD TRAUMAS

It is God's will for you and me to live an abundant life. 3 John 1:2, "Beloved, I wish above all things that thou mayest prosper and be in health, even as thy soul prospereth." There are three major areas of our lives that the Lord is concerned about prospering; our spirit, bodies, and souls. When we say we are warriors in life, this means that we are overcoming each and every obstacle set in our way. And to the greater degree of victorious living we expect to experience, the greater the challenge it becomes to withstand the things that come against us.

There can be nothing worse than a defeated Christian. We know too much, have been through too much, and expect too much from the Lord to sit idly by and let the devil wreck our lives. Throughout scriptures we see that the people of God had to fight the good of faith in order to overcome. Apostle Paul says in 1 Timothy 6:12, "Fight the good fight of faith, lay hold on eternal life, whereunto thou art also called, and hast professed a good profession before many witnesses." Our fight is a 'good' fight because it is a fixed one. We have already won but we must posture ourselves for the battle. We are told to put on the whole armor of God that we may stand against the wiles of the devil. We don't have to advance him or charge him but the fact that we are postured releases the Lord to war on our behalf. 2 Chronicles 20:17, "Ye shall not need to fight in this battle: set yourselves, stand ye still, and see the salvation of the LORD with you, O Judah and Jerusalem: fear not, nor be dismayed; to morrow go out against them: for the LORD will be with you."

Ask any psychiatrist where they prefer to begin with patient counseling and they may tell you that the earliest memory of the patient's childhood is where they would rather begin. Contrary to popular opinion, it's not so much what we are doing now that lays the foundation for our lives, but it's what building material our lives were made of that lays foundations in our lives. It's those foundations that to this day often determines how successful or not our lives can be. So we will begin studying our own personal lives from the very beginning. To understand the present you must study your past. If you want to know where you are going, look at where you came from. "A people without the knowledge of their past history, origin and culture is like a tree without roots", says Marcus Garvey.

"We cannot change our past. We can not change the fact that people act in a certain way. We can not change the inevitable. The only thing we can do is play on the one string we have, and that is our attitude", says Charles R. Swindoll.

The past may not necessarily dictate who we are but we most certainly determine who we become and no matter how hard our past was, we can always begin again. Your past does not define you but it does prepare you. "It's okay to look back at your past, just don't stare there", says Benjamin Dover. The more anger you hold in your heart towards your past, the less capable you are of loving your present. The past cannot be changed, forgotten, edited, or erased. It can only be accepted.

Let's take a brief look backwards

- ***Overcoming Childhood Obstacles***

For most of us, there were circumstances which

Delisa Lindsey

haunted us in our childhood. Perhaps we were abused, poor, abandoned, or bullied. Through any of those environments, our souls were affected. How have we allowed the presence and healing of God to permeate those areas? Have we exposed them to Him? Do we still feel the shame, the pain, and the hurt from those incidents or is God still healing us? Give yourself an honest evaluation. If you can't be true to anyone else, at least to thine own self be true.

The biblical characters Joseph and David both understood how to overcome childhood obstacles. Joseph was bullied and harassed by his older siblings. He was then ripped away from the loving arms of his father, Jacob and cast into a land filled with strange people, strange customs, and their strange gods. Read the biblical accounts of how they overcame. They allowed the Lord to process them through their pain to become better persons and not embittered by their circumstances. The same can apply to you if you are willing to forgive, release, let God heal you, and move on.

Romans 8:8, "For I consider that the sufferings of this present time are not worth comparing with the glory that is to be revealed to us."

- Revelation 21:4, "He will wipe away every tear from their eyes, and death shall be no more, neither shall there be mourning, nor crying, nor pain anymore, for the former things have passed away."
- Psalm 147:3, "He heals the brokenhearted and binds up their wounds."
- Psalm 34:18, "The Lord is near to the brokenhearted and saves the crushed in spirit."

Case Study

"A 30-year-old man whose mother sold him to two men when he was eight years old. The men took him to a different city, sexually abused and tortured him, then left him to die in a basement. He managed to escape, and was staggering, bleeding, down the street when a family driving by spotted him and took him to the police station. That family later adopted him, but those first eight years of his life have taken a toll. "[i]

Thoughts to Ponder:

How do you think this man's childhood affected him as an adult?

- Satan had a hand against this man from eight years

12/26/14

Delisa Lindsey

old, what would it take for him to be restored?

How would you pray for this victim of circumstance?

BIND + LOOSE
Let Him Confess and Denounce things
Repent
Forgive

- **Family Dynamics – Sibling Rivalry**   — Color — favored — Attentions

Sibling rivalry is the contention between sisters and brothers in a home. This can also occur more frequently among blended families. Competition, violence, greed, jealousy, and clamoring for attention are all common place in a home where there is sibling rivalry. Families will have disagreements that are normal occurrences of a group of two or more people living together for an extended period of time but what happens when living with family becomes an art of survival? How do you cope with living with siblings who compete with you, despise you, undermine you, tease you, and mistreat you? It is not easy but through God's grace He is able to deliver.

Answer →

Let's look at a famous Bible case that did not end well for a brother marked for cruelty by his brother. We will see that evil in the home is a very real phenomenon and is more common place than we may have ever realized.

"In Genesis 2, Cain is shown as a "tiller of soil" while Abel becomes the keeper of sheep. In the course of time,

① Abel, ② Joseph

Cain brought an offering of "fruit of the soil" (most likely an offering of crops), and Abel brought the healthiest, choicest firstling of his flock of sheep as his offering. The story goes on to show that God is very pleased with Abel's offering, but ultimately rejects Cain's. Cain is disheartened and God explains to Cain that if he is upset he merely needs to "do right" to be uplifted. Cain became jealous of God's approval of Abel, and instead of heading God's words Cain directs his anger towards Abel. Cain then lures his brother away and kills him.

There are a number or theories when it comes to finding the root of sibling jealousy and endless combinations of possible factors. In some cases maybe your brother was the first born and it was always obvious that he received the most love from your parents. Maybe he wasn't the first born, but was brilliant and extremely good-looking. Or maybe, you were the one the others were jealous of. But, researchers agree, no matter which side of the spectrum a person is on, those childhood feelings can manifest themselves into ugly resentment. God is referred to as "the Heavenly Father" constantly. I think it is clear that Cain envied Abel for his approval from God. In out of resentment and frustration, he was willing to kill his brother. "[ii]

The envy, bitterness, and resentment was so strong in the first family between brothers that it resulted in human civilization's first murder. Satan is still causing 'murders' today among brothers. Consider what the word of God has to say about the danger of hating our brothers. 1 John 3:15, "Whosoever hateth his brother is a murderer: and ye know that no murderer hath eternal life abiding in him." 1 John 2:11, "But he that hateth his brother is in darkness, and walketh in darkness, and knoweth not whither he goeth, because that darkness hath blinded his eyes." 1 John 4:20, "If a man say, I love God, and hateth his brother, he is a liar: for he that loveth not his brother whom he hath seen, how can he love God whom he hath not seen?"

"In the case of Joseph and his brothers, there was no "brotherly love." There was, however, envy and hatred. It would seem the dynamics of the family have an extreme effect on the relationship of siblings. Anger and resentment were propelled by agitation (Joseph's dreams), resulting in a horribly intense sibling rivalry." [iii]

1 Peter 2:17, "Honour all men. Love the brotherhood. Fear God. Honour the king."

Leviticus 19:17 You shall not hate your brother in your heart

Thoughts to Ponder :

How do we as parents watch for this spirit?

How do we cope with this spirit as siblings?

How has bitterness, envy, and resentment in family affected us?

- **Forgiving Parents**

"When you forgive, you in no way change the past - but you sure do change the future", says Bernard Meltzer.

It is God's perfect plan for children to be successfully reared by two loving and Godly parents. The enemy disturbed this plan from day one by instigating the first family fight, family violence, and domestic mayhem of which we have just studied. But how do you forgive a family member who has harmed you? More specifically, what if it was one of your parents who harmed you? What do you do if you were abused by your parents?

"The first step for someone who has been abused is

to be willing to forgive. This, too, will seem to be utterly impossible, especially for those who have suffered the worst kinds of abuse. Bitterness can sink into their souls, weighing them down like iron, yet there is nothing the Holy Spirit cannot soften and cleanse. With God all things are possible Mark 10:27. Our Lord understands our pain; He "was crucified in weakness, yet he lives by God's power" 2 Corinthians 13:4.

There is no need to fear being honest with God. If you find it difficult to forgive the wickedness of a parent's behavior, talk to God about it. It is true that unforgiveness is sin, but only deliberate unforgiveness, where we have set our hearts like flint and vowed that never again will we even consider forgiveness for those who have hurt us so badly. A child of God going to his Father for help with something he cannot do for himself will find not an angry, threatening God waiting to punish him, but a Father with a heart full of overwhelming love, compassion, mercy and a desire to help.

So, what does honoring an abusive parent look like in real life? Here are some practical tips: call your parent and listen, even though you've heard the same stories repeatedly. Remain quiet rather than defend yourself when hurtful things are said. Let go of expectations that your parent will ever be the parent you want him or her to be; replace your disappointment and sadness with acceptance of who the person is. Cultivate an attitude of compassion for the things your parent did right and express gratitude for even slight efforts to show love. Refrain from making disparaging remarks about your parent to other family members. Create safe boundaries so that you can reduce sinful temptations for you and your parent."[iv]

Psalm 27:10, "For my father and my mother have forsaken me, but the Lord will take me in."

Colossians 3:21, "Fathers, do not provoke your children, lest they become discouraged."

Isaiah 49:15, ""Can a woman forget her nursing child, that she should have no compassion on the son of her womb? Even these may forget, yet I will not forget you."

Thoughts to Ponder :

What was your relationship like with your parent(s)?
How has that impacted your life?
Was there ever anything you wanted to say to your parents and have not? Take a moment to journal it

privately and turn your thoughts into a prayer as you release the burdens of your heart. 1 Peter 5:7, "Casting all your care upon him; for he careth for you."

- **Abuse – Verbal, Physical, And Sexual**

"The Bible gives much practical advice on the subject of child-rearing. "Train up a child in the way he should go, even when he is old he will not depart from it," says the writer of Proverb 22:6. Parents are clearly cautioned to take steps to correct foolishness which "is bound up in the heart of a child," Prov. 22:15.

Parental discipline is essential, but some parents view these Scriptures as giving absolute control over their children. This is not true. God's Word should never be used as a license for abuse. Parents need to discipline their children, but they must keep their own emotions and actions in check, Eph. 6:4 and Col. 3:21. In God's eyes there simply is no justification for abuse.

If you have been the victim of abuse, you need to know that God has not abandoned you. He is "intimately acquainted" with all your ways Psalm 139:3. He knows your pain, and He has a plan for complete healing and restoration for your life. Consider these simple steps as you seek the Father's healing.

1. <u>Face the abuse</u>. The shame associated with abuse is unbearable. You can hide the pain for a season, but eventually, the wounds will surface. But take comfort, for God knows the horror that you have unjustly endured see Psalm 139 and Matt. 10:29-31. Ask God for the strength to face your nightmare of abuse.

2. <u>Forgive and release</u>. As difficult as it may sound, you need to begin by forgiving the perpetrator for his or her actions against you. It may seem impossible, but the consequences of un-forgiveness can produce even further destruction, 2 Samuel 13:23-29. Instead, ask God to give you the grace you need to forgive, 1 Samuel 1:15-17, Psalm 42:3-4, and Psalm 62:8.

3. <u>Seek shelter</u>. If you are still in an abusive situation, immediately seek shelter. Consider turning to family members, your church family, or perhaps authorities if necessary. Ultimately, rest in God's shelter. Turn to His Word (the Psalms offer much encouragement for the downcast).

4. <u>Move on</u>. Once you have taken steps to forgive, ask God to help you pick up the pieces, and seek again the abundant life in Jesus that He has for you (John 10:10). Press on and leave the past to God (Phil. 3:13-14)."[v]

Abuse affects our lives for years after the actual event(s) have occurred. Physical abuse results in fear of authority figures, depression, low self esteem, low self worth, and addictions to say the least. Sexual abuse results in promiscuity, flirtatiousness, uncontrolled sex drive, frigidity, fear, anger, guilt, addictive behaviors, and anxiety. Verbal abuse is the silent blow to one's ego.

2
OVERCOMING SEXUAL ABUSE

"...I started to realize how many great things could happen by confronting the things that scare you most." - David Archuleta

"Nothing is better for self-esteem than survival."
— Martha Gellhorn

"When you feel humiliated or things like that, you either use it as fuel to change or you get covered by it." — Diane Von Furstenberg

"Sometimes there's a fire in your life and you ask God,
"Lord, let me go around the fire." And God says, "No."
Then you ask, "Lord, then let me go over the fire."
And God says, "No." Then you ask,
"Well Lord, please let me go under the fire."

And God says, "No. Go through the fire and I'll be with you." — Lydia Thornton

"The beautiful thing about setbacks is they introduce us to our strengths." — Robin Sharma

"Nobody looks good in their darkest hour. But it's those hours that make us what we are. We stand strong, or we cower. We emerge victorious, tempered by our trials, or fractured by a permanent damning fault line." — Karen Marie Moning

I often say that the Bible has more drama recorded than any soap opera. It is hard to understand why people have such a hard time studying the Word of God. It is so rich and chock full of all types of situations that both the Godly and ungodly have had to face and through their testimonies, we learn how to overcome. From incest, rape, adultery, fornication, even orgies, the Bible records them all. One story in particular we will review in terms of a rape victim is in the life of Tamar.

Tamar was David's daughter and the victim of forced sexual relations by her very own half brother, Amnon. Let's take a look at 2 Samuel 13:11-14, "And when she had brought them unto him to eat, he took hold of her, and said unto her, Come lie with me, my sister. And she answered him, Nay, my brother, do not force me; for no such thing ought to be done in Israel: do not thou this folly. And I, whither shall I cause my shame to go? and as for thee, thou shalt be as one of the fools in Israel. Now therefore, I pray thee, speak unto the king; for he will not withhold me from thee. Howbeit he would not hearken unto her voice: but, being stronger than she, forced her, and lay with her."

To appreciate the full story I recommend you read the entire chapter of 2 Samuel 13.

How devastating do you think it was for a young girl to be forced into sexual relations with her own brother? Tamar loved Amnon as a brother, not as man, but an evil desire grew within him that coupled with the wicked counsel of his 'friend', Jonadab, forced him upon his virgin sister to sexually molest her. Let's look at the mental effects she suffered as a result of this heinous incident. 2 Samuel 13:19, "And Tamar put ashes on her head, and rent her garment of divers colours that was on her, and laid her hand on her head, and went on crying." 2 Samuel 13:20b, "So Tamar remained desolate in her brother

Absalom's house." The Hebrew word for desolate is *shamem* and it means, "be appalled, stun, stupefy, be awestruck, causing horror, be astounded, to cause oneself desolation, cause oneself ruin".[vi]

"To cast her out now, a violated woman, was worse than raping her, since it meant the crime continued. She could never marry or have children, never have a normal life. As far as the people around her were concerned, she would be a used object, unwanted, an outcast.

Amnon ignored her words. He was without pity or remorse. He had his servant literally throw her out of the room. He would not even use her name: 'Put this woman out of my presence, and bolt the door after her.'" [vii]

Numerous spirits entered into the House of David after this horrid act occurred. Once sexual immorality entered the family line, demons of rage, murder, insurrection, and despair had a legal right to attack the House of David. Why did these spirits have the right to attack the House of God if only Amnon and Tamar were involved? Because once the issue was brought to David's attention, (being the head of the family) he neglected in handling the matter according to the word of God.

Deuteronomy 22:25-27, "But if a man find a betrothed damsel in the field, and the man force her, and lie with her: then the man only that lay with her shall die: But unto the damsel thou shalt do nothing; there is in the damsel no sin worthy of death: for as when a man riseth against his neighbour, and slayeth him, even so is this matter: For he found her in the field, and the betrothed damsel cried, and there was none to save her."

David was supposed to put Amnon to death but he did not. When David neglected his part, Absalom rose up to defend his sister's honor. Disgusted with his father for turning a deaf ear to his sister's complaint, murder, violence, hatred, and rage entered Absalom. Not only did he murder his brother Amnon, but he also made a concerted effort to usurp David's kingdom and divide the loyalty of the people. This forbidden act resulted in his own murder and David's decline into depression after losing Absalom.

Let this be a lesson. When there is the act of incest or rape in the household, the abuser must be brought to justice. The victim must be protected unlike as in the case of Tamar and so many other silent sufferers today. The criminal must be brought to justice.

John 16:33, "I have said these things to you, that in me you may have peace. In the world you will have tribulation. But take heart; I have overcome the world."

1 John 5:4, "For everyone who has been born of God overcomes the world. And this is the victory that has overcome the world—our faith."

1 John 4:4, "Little children, you are from God and have overcome them, for he who is in you is greater than he who is in the world."

Revelation 3:21, "The one who conquers, I will grant him to sit with me on my throne, as I also conquered and sat down with my Father on his throne."

Your past is what God is using to sensitive you to the needs of others. It is what makes your heart beat when encountering others who are going through what you have gone through. It's the wisdom and advice you give to a rape victim, a molestation victim, or a sexually abused child. You know the signs to look for. You know how to discern the neighbor who is afraid to step outside of her door. And you have the tools they need to give them the help they deserve to trust and love again.

Our past does not prevent us from being used by the Lord. His Blood washes, cleanses, and sanctifies. When He saved us, He saved us from our past and gave us a future. In Christ, we have a brand new start. Philippians 4:13, "I can do all things through Christ which strengtheneth me." Our pasts cannot hold us, cannot control us, and cannot bind us. We are not products of our past but we are 'new creations' in Christ. 2 Corinthians 5:17, "Therefore if any man be in Christ, he is a new creature: old things are passed away; behold, all things are become new." Isaiah 41:8, ""Forget the former things; do not dwell on the past." Ezekiel 36:26, "I will give you a new heart and put a new spirit in you; I will remove from you your heart of stone and give you a heart of flesh." Revelation 21:5, "He who was seated on the throne said, "I am making everything new!" Then he said, "Write this down, for these words are trustworthy and true.""

There were many recorded in the Word of God whom God used despite their past. Apostle Peter was used mightily AFTER He denied the Lord three times. In fact, Simon Peter preached his greatest message and had his greatest ministry after he denied the Lord. Moses killed an Egyptian but God used him for His glory. Samson was a fornicator but God used him to punish the Philistines. Abraham lied on two occasions but he is called the Father of Faith. Jacob, whose name means deceiver, was in fact a deceiver but he wrestled with God and received a name change that is a blessing to every nation upon the earth today. You, with all of your issues, your marks and scars, are being mightily used of the Lord despite who touched you, abused you, or abandoned you. You are God's masterpiece and don't ever let a devil from the past tell you otherwise.

Use what happened to you to better you. Channel your pain and hurt into that which benefits others, enhances their lives, and brings Glory to God. You can sit bitter or sit better. The choice is yours but God is willing to help you take 'that' thing to another level of victory in your life and for the sake of multitudes of others.

Thoughts to Ponder

Gather the fragmented parts of your life back into one whole piece. Make sure you are whole in Christ. Reach back into your past and stop at the ages where life impacted you the most. Remember the pain, the shame, the hurt, the humiliation and write a prayer to yourself. In other words, as you picture yourself at the age of shame or pain, pray for 'that' child. After you have written your prayer, speak comforting verses of scripture over 'that' child, the little you. And finally, prophesy over your young life.

Take For Example:

Prayer-

Father, in the name of Jesus, I pray for 'Mary'. I pray that you heal her of the shame of sexual abuse. Forgive the ones who touched her inappropriately and make them aware of the pain they have caused her (assuming that they are still alive). May she know that You are not mad at her for what happened and that though You don't approve, You will always be there to strengthen her through this. Let this thing not destroy her but build her in Jesus name. Amen.

Scriptures -

Deuteronomy 31:8

The LORD himself goes before you and will be with you; he will never leave you nor forsake you. Do not be afraid; do not be discouraged."

Psalm 34:17

The righteous cry out, and the LORD hears them; he delivers them from all their troubles.

Prophecy -

Mary, you will rise from the ashes of defeat. You are going through a storm right now but God promises to deliver you. It is rough to stand and believe God loves you but He does. And when you come out of this, you are going to see how your pain is going to bless multitudes. Be strong for the Lord is your portion.

3

OVERCOMING THE LOVE OF MONEY

Nothing much affects our life like our money. It determines where we live, what we drive, how our homes are furnished, which clothes we wear, our eating habits, and our outlook on life in general. People will lie for money, kill for money, and cheat for money. Money can bring out the best in us or the worst. 1 Timothy 6:10 says, "For the love of money is the root of all kinds of evil. And some people, craving money, have wandered from the true faith and pierced themselves with many sorrows."

Money is not evil in and of itself, but it can bring out the worst of the best of us. Many a scandal has been the result of the love of money. In fact, in Charlotte, NC, right now, we are dealing with political corruption as it pertains to money. So although we all NEED money to survive, it is unhealthy and unwise to form an attachment to money. There is a dark side to money that we need to remain aware of. The evil spirit behind money is called, mammon. Jesus alluded to the evil spirit of mammon four times in scripture.

    Matthew 6:4, "No man can serve two masters: for either he will hate the one, and love the other; or else he will hold to the one, and despise the other. Ye cannot serve God and mammon."

    Luke 16:9, "And I say unto you, Make to yourselves friends of the mammon of unrighteousness; that, when ye fail, they may receive you into everlasting habitations."

    Luke 16:13, "No servant can serve two masters: for either he will hate the one, and love the other; or else he will hold to the one, and despise the other. Ye cannot serve God and mammon."

    Luke 16:11, "If therefore ye have not been faithful in the unrighteous mammon, who will commit to your trust the true riches?"

    Mammon in the Hebrew tongue is "*mamōnas*", and it means, "*the god of riches*".[viii] Mammon means riches. Mammon says you don't need God, you need money. Mammon is an evil spirit, the spirit of Antichrist. God is the source of your blessings. He will multiply your money as long as you honor Him with it first. Mammon is a liar. The Lord says you cannot serve God and Mammon. It's either God or Mammon. Mammon says you cannot provide for your family without me. If you had more Mammon or money you will be better off.

Money isn't evil. It's the worship of it that is evil. Use your money for good. Submit and redeem your money to God and let Him rule your resources.

Be a good steward of money. Come to terms with the simple fact that God has all the resources we need as He blesses us we need to bless Him in return. The good steward gets more. Matthew 25:28-29, "Therefore take the talent from him and give it to the one who has ten. For the one who has will be given more, and he will have more than enough. But the one who does not have, even what he has will be taken from him.".

Be faithful in your giving remembering that God owns it all. It's His to begin with. Give what belongs to Him so that He can multiply what belongs to you. To simplify your worship in giving, be a good steward and give generously. Whatever you do, don't let mammon entrap you with selfishness. Selfishness promotes self! Mammon will say to you, "Protect yourself, take care of yourself, and look out for yourself." But the Lord is saying in 1 Peter 5:7, "Casting all your care upon him; for he careth for you."

There are three levels of giving. Tithes, love offerings, and extravagant offerings. Tithes are 10 percent of your increase. Genesis 14:20, "And blessed be the most high God, which hath delivered thine enemies into thy hand. And he gave him tithes of all." The heavens opened in Genesis 15:1, "After these things the word of the LORD came unto Abram in a vision, saying, Fear not, Abram: I am thy shield, and thy exceeding great reward." Get past this first level and the gates of heaven will open and you will have so much you will have to give more away.

Love offerings are those funds which you purpose in your heart to give which is beside your tithe. 2 Corinthians 9:7, "Every man according as he purposeth in his heart, so let him give; not grudgingly, or of necessity: for God loveth a cheerful giver." Exodus 25:2, "Speak unto the children of Israel, that they bring me an offering: of every man that giveth it willingly with his heart ye shall take my offering". Exodus 35:21, "And they came, every one whose heart stirred him up, and every one whom his spirit made willing, and they brought the LORD'S offering to the work of the tabernacle of the congregation, and for all his service, and for the holy garments."

Your tithe is a requirement but your love offering is what you decide to give based on what you feel in your heart. The next level of matured giving is the extravagant form of giving. The extravagant offering is far beyond the tithe and love offering. It can be compared to the Father who offered Jesus for the sins of the world. John 3:16, " For God so loved the world, that he gave his only begotten Son, that whosoever believeth in him should not perish, but have everlasting life." You may hear many refer to this type of offering as a 'seed'. It is an offering on purpose to achieve a specific harvest. Matthew 26:7, "There came unto him a woman having an alabaster box of very precious ointment, and poured it on his head, as he sat at meat." The woman depicted here gave an extravagant offering. It turns Heaven's attention to you and brings you extraordinary favor and blessings. Let's also consider Solomon. 2 Chronicles 7:5, "And king Solomon offered a sacrifice of twenty and two thousand oxen, and an hundred and twenty thousand sheep: so the king and all the people dedicated the house of God." The heavens opened up for Solomon as recorded in 2 Chronicles 7:12, "And the LORD appeared to Solomon by night, and said unto him, I have heard thy prayer, and have chosen this place to myself for an house of sacrifice."

As you can see, mammon is the direct enemy that stops in our way to block us from blessing the Lord. When we allow mammon to block us, we also block God's hands from blessing us. We all stand in need of God's blessings so it behooves us to find out what it takes to keep the gates of Heaven open over our life and maintain them that way. Once you find favor in the sight of the Lord, you ought not ever lose it.

4

WWJD? (WHAT WOULD JESUS DO?)

The Lord Jesus was not money hungry during His earthly ministry. He was no 'prosperity preacher' in the sense that His life was governed by money and lots of it. Quite the contrary, Jesus made of Himself 'no reputation'. He was born in a lowly manger, an animal stable, and was raised by a poor family. The family's offering of two turtledoves were an indication of their financial state. Turtle doves were the poor man's offering.

> Leviticus 5:7, ""Anyone who cannot afford a lamb is to bring two doves or two young pigeons to the LORD as a penalty for their sin--one for a sin offering and the other for a burnt offering."
>
> Luke 2:24, "They also offered a sacrifice according to what is specified in the Law of the Lord: "a pair of turtledoves or two young pigeons.""

Jesus was raised in Nazareth. Can anything good come out of Nazareth? (John 1:46) Nazareth was a small unimportant town. The population there was poor and relatively small. It paled in comparison to the other bustling cities of commerce such as Jerusalem or Capernaum. It was similar to the hick towns we have today where there is one stoplight; the ones comedians joke that if you winked as you passed by you will miss it. I would say that Nazareth in our time would be the town where there is no Wal-Mart! What good could come out of small nothing of a town like that? (smile)

"Nazareth was a village of no more than 500 in the days when Jesus grew up there. Nazareth is about 16 miles southwest of the Sea of Galilee; it is not near the Mediterranean Sea and would not be on a lot of travel routes. It is evident why Nazareth would easily be despised in the eyes of others: it is in the backwoods or out in the sticks, a small village. In the eyes of more educated and urban Jews, the Nazarenes would have been judged as ignorant at best and perhaps as simple-minded sinners at worst."[ix] We see that not only was Jesus born into poverty, but he was raised in poverty.

Let's look at His adult life.

Luke 9:58, "And Jesus said unto him, Foxes have

holes, and birds of the air have nests; but the Son of man hath not where to lay his head." Unlike the religious leaders of His day, Jesus was relatively homeless. He had to depend on the welfare and love offerings from the people He served. He did not come to the earth to build a mansion, own a fleet of cars, and live a life of luxury. Jesus understood like Apostle Paul did that the more physical things we have, the more time we must spend attending to them. Paul says in 1 Corinthians 7:7, "But I wish everyone were single, just as I am. Yet each person has a special gift from God, of one kind or another."

Jesus was not distracted by cleaning the gutters or mowing the lawn. He knew that He only had 33 years on the earth to impact it for the Kingdom of God, therefore He knew better than to serve Mammon and bow down to the devil. Matthew 4:9, "And saith unto him, All these things will I give thee, if thou wilt fall down and worship me."

The funny thing is that many say they want to be like Jesus but careful observation of their lives actually reveals that many are NOTHING like Jesus. Jesus did not have a church building. He didn't have steeples, padded benches, or even the luxury of central heating and air. In fact, Jesus only spent a short amount of time in the Temple. He preferred the streets where He met ordinary people dealing with the challenges of life and He ministered to them every day, not just on the Sabbath. He depended on the hospitality and open hearts of those He ministered to minister to His physical needs of shelter, food, and clothing. People gave but it was the women who were more liberal in their giving than men. There is something about women having compassion on someone in need. Luke 8:3, "Joanna, the wife of Chuza, Herod's business manager; Susanna; and many others who were contributing from their own resources to support Jesus and his disciples." Even our modern research has found that women are liberal in their giving than men. "According to a recent study by the Women's Philanthropy Institute at the University of Indiana, women are as much as 40% more likely to donate than men. What's more, women at nearly every income level are better givers. Not only do they give more often; they also tend to donate more. For example, the study found that a female-headed household with a family income of at least $103,000 is likely to give to charities, on average, nearly $1,910, or $1,000 more a year than a similar household in which a man controls the checkbook."[x]

Thoughts to Ponder:

Describe the type of ministry the Lord Jesus would oversee today if He were to return to human form?

After having read about Mammon, consider the relationship you have with your money. How would you evaluate it based on what you know now?

Have you ever been looked down upon by others because of your financial status or have you looked down upon others because they didn't meet your status? Explain.

5

OVERCOMING THE BEAST OF DEBT

Mortgage. Rent. Utilities. Insurance. Taxes. Vehicle Financing. What do these things have in common? They are all forms of debt. Debt is defined as, "Something that is owed or that one is bound to pay to or perform for another: a liability or obligation to pay or render something." Romans 13:8, "Owe no one anything, except to love each other, for the one who loves another has fulfilled the law." While the Lord does not forbid debt, He certainly warns against it. He also frowns upon those who take advantage of the poor by charging excessive interest on their debt. Proverbs 28:8, "He that by usury and unjust gain increaseth his substance, he shall gather it for him that will pity the poor." This verse is saying that the person who charged exorbitant interest and gained much will in actuality lose it to the ONE who has pity on the poor. In other words, God, Himself will rob the one who is robbing the poor.

In Moses' day, lenders were forbidden to charge

interest to the poor. Leviticus 25:35-38, "If your brother becomes poor and cannot maintain himself with you, you shall support him as though he were a stranger and a sojourner, and he shall live with you. Take no interest from him or profit, but fear your God, that your brother may live beside you. You shall not lend him your money at interest, nor give him your food for profit. I am the Lord your God, who brought you out of the land of Egypt to give you the land of Canaan, and to be your God." These laws were enacted to protect the poor from becoming poorer and from being taken advantage of by the wealthier.

Although we are warned against debt, certain types of debt are essential. It will take the wisdom of God and temperance, a fruit of Holy Spirit, to live a financially stable life. It is not easy to do that. We are surrounded by bigger, better, and more, more, more. Many of us do not budget, are careless, overspend, and are just one paycheck from poverty. The Lord wants to break the burden of debt from us but we must comply with Him fully in order to so. This may mean obeying Him in areas we have been accustomed to being disobedient in. In other words, it's time to lay Isaac on the altar in order to receive the promise. Ready for the burn?

Warriors in Life

I have taught previously from Genesis 2:10-14 that God has granted us access to 4 rivers. These rivers are resources to provide for us and to sustain our households. One of the first keys to getting out debt is labor intensive efforts; we must connect to our streams of income. God does not work for us. We must work for ourselves and then He will bless the fruit of our hands. 2 Thessalonians 3:10, "For even when we were with you, this we commanded you, that if any would not work, neither should he eat." Genesis 2:15, "And the LORD God took the man, and put him into the garden of Eden to dress it and to keep it." From both illustrations we see that it is imperative for man to work. God created us to work and He gives us wisdom to sustain ourselves with the fruit of our labor. Psalm 1:3, "And he shall be like a tree planted by the rivers of water, that bringeth forth his fruit in his season; his leaf also shall not wither; and whatsoever he doeth shall prosper."

Notwithstanding being handicapped, aged, or otherwise unable to work, the Father expects His children to work and to do so diligently. Proverbs 10:4, "He becometh poor that dealeth with a slack hand: but the hand of the diligent maketh rich." Matthew 9:37, 'Then saith he unto his disciples, The harvest truly is plenteous, but the labourers are few." The Lord expounded that there is so much work to do but so few are willing to roll up their sleeves to get it done. He made that statement 2,000 years ago. Can you imagine what He would say to us now? I shudder to think!!

God gave us His work ethic to be productive and to sustain our families. He became the first example of a laborer when He worked six days out of the week and THEN rested and blessed His rest. Genesis 2:2, "And on the seventh day God ended his work which he had made; and he rested on the seventh day from all his work which he had made." Many have made a doctrine out of the seventh day but the number 7 means, 'completion'. In other words, the Lord did not stop working until His work was completed or finished. Remember this famous saying? John 19:30, "When Jesus therefore had received the vinegar, he said, It is finished: and he bowed his head, and gave up the ghost." Jesus RESTED. He gave up the ghost or RESTED from His earthly labor. The problem that is occurring in our modern times is that many are resting from their labor when they haven't completed their work! Who told you to stop working? Who told you to rest?

According to the Sleep Foundation, the adult body only needs approximately 7 hours to rest or sleep!![xi] There goes that 7 again!! If there are 24 hours in a day, that means two –thirds of our day should be directed toward something productive. Bear with me, we are going somewhere. We are still talking about getting out of debt but right now we are laying foundations in wisdom to show you how to win God's heart so you can attract His favor.

Proverbs 6:6, "Go to the ant, thou sluggard; consider her ways, and be wise:" The Lord frowns on lazy people. Romans 12:11, "Not slothful in business; fervent in spirit; serving the Lord". When Jesus called the disciples, He called working men, men of industry, and men who could (in the words of my overseer, Apostle Ivory Hopkins), "Get 'er done"! Nowhere in scripture do you find the Lord partnering with anyone who was lazy and shiftless. Proverbs 12:27, "The slothful man roasteth not that which he took in hunting: but the substance of a diligent man is precious." The Bible talks about the lazy man who was too lazy to cook the food they caught!! Proverbs 13:4, "The soul of the sluggard desireth, and hath nothing: but the soul of the diligent shall be made fat." A lazy person is always in need but won't do anything of their own accord toward getting those needs met. God will NEVER show forth His favor in finance to a person of this kind.

Consider this, even Gideon was full of fear but because he kept working despite his fear, the Lord prophesied to him a new name and changed his life forever. Judges 6:12, "And the angel of the LORD appeared unto him, and said unto him, The LORD is with thee, thou mighty man of valour."

Let's deal with our debt. Who do you owe? Make a list of your creditors and the amounts you are indebted to them. Nothing magical is going to happen when you do that so calm down, but in order to take the beast of debt down, you must first confront him. Now, set that aside and turn your attention to what your income is. If you don't have income, prepare yourself to receive a steady source of income. Why am I saying this? I am speaking prophetically to you but I am also helping you to align yourself in the will of God. The Father is obligated to His word. What I am doing is teaching you how to attract divine favor. (See my YouTube message entitled, "How To Attract the Divine Favor Of God", that corresponds to this topic at http://youtu.be/sp0_QjRz5s0.) When you turn to face your 'Goliath', your debt, and you have the 'stones' in your hand – a work ethic, God will step into the fight with you.

2 Timothy 1:7, "For God hath not given us the spirit of fear; but of power, and of love, and of a sound mind." 1 John 4:18, "There is no fear in love; but perfect love casteth out fear: because fear hath torment. He that feareth is not made perfect in love." Fear causes us to lie to our bill collectors. Fear causes us to have our children lie to our bill collectors for us. Fear imagines the worst if we 'took that call.' If we are to live debt free, we must cast out fear by the love of God. There is a place of favor in the Lord where your bill collectors will deal kindly with you. If you would be honest with explaining to them your circumstances, they may have options to help you. If you would work along with your creditors and not play the 'bait and switch' game with them, God will assign a person whose heart He has touched to help you but you must show good faith. You must walk in the wisdom of the Lord as it pertains to YOUR finances.

Ok, let's talk about your finances. Yes, it's time to dig in your business because many of you don't even realize that you already have what you need to become debt free but as an unwise steward are blowing it. You can't keep up with the Joneses when you're in debt. You can't dine out and entertain yourself every day when you are in debt. You have responsibilities. You have to set your priorities. First, of all, stop complaining about what you don't have because you are licensing the enemy of lack to attach himself to what you do have. Change your professions. Philippians 4:19, "But my God shall supply all your need according to his riches in glory by Christ Jesus." Psalm 23:1, "The LORD is my shepherd; I shall not want." 2 Corinthians 9:8, "And God is able to make all grace abound toward you; that ye, always having all sufficiency in all things, may abound to every good work:" You DO have enough to provide for your house, you just need the mind of God to show you how to manifest it from the spiritual realm into the natural and being disobedient to God in your finances is NOT HELPING you at all.

Deuteronomy 8:18, "But thou shalt remember the LORD thy God: for it is he that giveth thee power to get wealth, that he may establish his covenant which he sware unto thy fathers, as it is this day." 1 Samuel 2:7, "The LORD maketh poor, and maketh rich: he bringeth low, and lifteth up." Who gives you power to get wealth people of God? The Lord!! Who makes one poor and the other rich? The Lord!! When you waste your resources or squander what the Lord makes available to you, you dig yourself into a very deep pit that you can't easily climb out of. You need God's favor over your money. You need

Him to make available that promotion on your job. You need Him to open doors of gainful employment. You need Him to arrange your schedule on your second job that you can still have family time. (Yes, a part time job if that is what you need to eliminate your debt.) Your bills are not going to vanish away. The Lord is going to wash your sins in the Blood, not your bills. Your bills are your responsibility and you have work to get them paid. There is no Holy Ghost takeover at the Credit Bureau to clean up your credit. You made the mess but with God's help and a good credit repair program, you will get it cleaned up. Yes, you will.

A woman had a debt. The debtors were coming to take her son. She was a widow and had no means of paying off her husband's loans but one thing she did have was a relationship with a prophet. She had his favor and God had his ear for her situation. The prophet did not call out, "Abra Cadabra… whoosh.. bill be gone!" No. The prophet told her to BORROW containers and fill them with what she had in her house. What do you have in your house? Not your three-bedroom house. I'm talking about you –the flesh house! The widowed woman used those containers, filled them oil, and sold them for a profit. Under the direction of the prophet, this widowed woman opened the very first oil company. As she made money, she paid off her debts. (The marketplace prophet Joseph opened the first banking system in Egypt with Pharoah's money!)

"Elisha readily received a poor widow's complaint. Those that leave their families under a load of debt know not what trouble they cause. It is the duty of all who profess to follow the Lord, while they trust to God for daily bread, not to tempt him by carelessness or extravagance, nor to contract debts; for nothing tends more to bring reproach upon the gospel, or distresses their families more when they are gone. Elisha put the widow in a way to pay her debt, and to maintain herself and her family. This was done by miracle, but so as to show what is the best method to assist those who are in distress, which is, to help them to improve by their own industry what little they have. The oil, sent by miracle, continued flowing as long as she had empty vessels to receive it. We are never straitened in God, or in the riches of his grace; all our straitness is in ourselves. It is our faith that fails, not his promise. He gives more than we ask: were there more vessels, there is enough in God to fill them; enough for all, enough for each; and the Redeemer's all-sufficiency will only be stayed from the supplying the wants of sinners and saving their souls, when no more apply to him for salvation. The widow must pay her debt with the money she received for her oil. Though her creditors were too hard with her, yet they must be paid, even before she made any provision for her children. It is one of the main laws of the Christian religion, that we pay every just debt, and give every one his own, though we leave ever so little for ourselves; and this, not of constraint, but for conscience to sake. Those who bear an honest mind, cannot with pleasure eat their daily bread, unless it be their own bread. She and her children must live upon the rest; that is, upon the money received for the oil, with which they must put themselves into a way to get an honest livelihood. We cannot now expect miracles, yet we may expect mercies, if we wait on God, and seek to him. Let widows in particular depend upon him. He that has all hearts in his hand, can, without a miracle, send as effectual a supply. (2Ki 4:8-17)"[xii]

Does God have respect of persons? Romans 2:11, "For there is no respect of persons with God." What He did for that widow He will do for you but you must have an ear to hear what the Spirit of the Lord is saying to you. Don't panic over your financial situation because then you partner with a demon of fear which shuts God out. Look to the Lord for financial counsel, inquire of His prophets and advisors and don't just LISTEN to their counsel, OBEY it. Do you want my advice? (You ask great questions!) Make up your mind that you are getting out of debt and BELIEVE IT. Take control of your money. Don't let Mammon run your life. Shop when you NEED to and even then, pray, ask the Lord for favor with discounts and bargains. Maintain what you have and take care of it. Ignore what everyone else is doing. Mind your own financial affairs. Have patience. Becoming debt free takes time. After all, look at how many years you spent burying yourself in debt. Tithe – we will talk about that later (yep, we are going there). Don't buy anything else that you can't pay cash for if you can help it. Downsize and be content with living at your river of resource. Elijah was content at the brook eating from dirty birds. 1 Kings 17:5-6, "So he went and did according unto the word of the LORD: for he went and dwelt by the brook Cherith, that is before Jordan. And the ravens brought him bread and flesh in the morning, and bread and flesh in the evening; and he drank of the brook." You may not have what you want while you are being processed through your debt but God will provide for you to meet your needs.

When your increase comes, for it will if you are

aligning yourself in the Word, use your money wisely. If you need someone to be accountable to, find that person. Pray over your money when you FIRST receive it and bless it. Honor the Lord with it and thank Him for it. Before you buy anything or pay anyone, sacrifice unto the Lord. Give Him what He tells you to give because the enemy is going to wear your mind out with everything you need and everything you want. Shut him up and listen to Holy Spirit. After you have sacrificed, ask Holy Spirit to show you how to use what is remaining. Before you shop for anything, eat out, or buy a movie ticket, pay your bills. If you cannot pay them in full, make payment arrangements. If you have to, pay them in halves. God will grant you wisdom in this. Reduce your electrical usage to lower your bill. Look for ways to reduce your monthly expenses. Use more sunlight by opening curtains and blinds and use lower wattage light bulbs. Eat dinner as a unit once it is finished to restrict costs associated with microwave reheating. Iron clothes at one time and not every day, several times a day. Dry clothes with wisdom. Air dry if you must. Use the Laundromat. Turn off the faucet when not in use. These are all ways to lower your monthly expenses and yet, Holy Spirit can show you so many more ways if you will listen to Him. Let Holy Spirit reprogram your thinking as it pertains to your money and you will see the Glory of God in your finances.

Thoughts to Ponder:

Make a list of 6 things you have done in the past year in your finances that you hear Holy Spirit telling you that you must change.

Make a list of 6 things you feel led to do now that will help improve your financial wellbeing.

What financial advice would you give to the next generation?

6

OVERCOMING STINGINESS

(ARE YOU A GIVER OR A TAKER?)

When you are a regular giver to the work of the ministry, God obligates Himself to you. Malachi 3:10, "Bring ye all the tithes into the storehouse, that there may be meat in mine house, and prove me now herewith, saith the LORD of hosts, if I will not open you the windows of heaven, and pour you out a blessing, that there shall not be room enough to receive it." In this text, the Lord promises to open windows of blessings upon the giver. I know we hear this verse every week but there are volumes of prophetic promises locked within just this passage alone. Remember, we are talking about being Warriors in Life in our Finances? We must learn how to overcome every evil spirit attaching itself to our finances and identify and displace the ones that are attacking them once our money is released. (See my book, Displacing Demonic Gate Watchers' Chapter on Demons at the Financial Gate for more insight). Partnering with the Lord in finance is an insurance policy that none of us can afford to be without.

Keep in mind that in the Old Testament the Law required the tithe but in the New Testament we are obligated not just to tithe but to give cheerfully. God doesn't want legislated giving under Grace. He doesn't want anything forced or coerced. He requires us to listen to Holy Spirit to give and on many instances that amount can be significantly more than a tithe. We now use the tithe as a rule of thumb to give, but by no means is it supposed to be the standard in giving. Plainly, in the Old Testament, we tithed based on the Law. In the New Covenant, we tithe based on Love. The latter cannot be measured.

John 3:16, "For God so loved the world, that he gave his only begotten Son, that whosoever believeth in him should not perish, but have everlasting life." God, the Father demonstrated what the tithe looks like under Grace. It is giving based on love. The Father planted His Word, His Son, Himself, in the earth and FULLY expected that Seed to prosper and yield Him and abundant harvest. Jesus, being the Tithe, the First Fruit, was placed in the womb of a woman (church) and gave birth (seed harvested) to a work that would OPEN windows that we could access Heaven. Does this sound familiar to Malachi 3:10? John 14:3, "And if I go and prepare a place for you, I will come again, and receive you unto myself; that where I am, there ye may be also." Just as the tithe attracts the Lord's presence, Jesus, the Tithe, brings us into the Lord's presence. As a matter of fact, God does not receive us if we don't come to Him through Jesus!! John 14:6, "Jesus saith unto him, I am the way, the truth, and the life: no man cometh unto the Father, but by me." Jesus is the way to Heaven, the only way and our tithe, offerings, and sacrifices are the ONLY way we can receive those types of open Heavens in Jesus name.

> Leviticus 9:24, "And there came a fire out from before the LORD, and consumed upon the altar the burnt offering and the fat: which when all the people saw, they shouted, and fell on their faces."
>
> Judges 13:19-20, "So Manoah took a kid with a meat offering, and offered it upon a rock unto the LORD: and the angel did wondrously; and Manoah and his wife looked on. For it came to pass, when the flame went up toward heaven from off the altar, that the angel of the LORD ascended in the flame of the altar. And Manoah and his wife looked on it, and fell on their faces to the ground."
>
> Judges 6:20- 21, "And the angel of God said unto him, Take the flesh and the unleavened cakes, and lay them upon this rock, and pour out the broth.

And he did so. Then the angel of the LORD put forth the end of the staff that was in his hand, and touched the flesh and the unleavened cakes; and there rose up fire out of the rock, and consumed the flesh and the unleavened cakes. Then the angel of the LORD departed out of his sight."

1 Kings 18:24, "And call ye on the name of your gods, and I will call on the name of the LORD: and the God that answereth by fire, let him be God. And all the people answered and said, It is well spoken."

2 Chronicles 7:1, "Now when Solomon had made an end of praying, the fire came down from heaven, and consumed the burnt offering and the sacrifices; and the glory of the LORD filled the house."

Do you get the point? When the offerings of the Lord were presented to Him and He was pleased with the people's sacrifice, the Heavens opened and He poured out Glory, Power, Clouds, Smoke, and Fire. Your giving to the Lord is NO SMALL THING. The enemy has deceived many in the Body of Christ in the area of their giving. He has seduced them into high interest loans, excess, and waste that by the time they come before the Lord, they show up as beggars; empty handed. They come looking instead of giving. This is not characteristic of a Warrior in Life in Finance. These kinds have been beguiled by satan and not only is satan robbing them but God is robbing them too. Haggai 1:6, "Ye have sown much, and bring in little; ye eat, but ye have not enough; ye drink, but ye are not filled with drink; ye clothe you, but there is none warm; and he that earneth wages earneth wages to put it into a bag with holes." Deuteronomy 28:38, "Thou shalt carry much seed out into the field, and shalt gather but little in; for the locust shall consume it." Jeremiah 12:13, "My people have planted wheat but are harvesting thorns. They have worn themselves out, but it has done them no good. They will harvest a crop of shame because of the fierce anger of the LORD."[xiii] Isaiah 5:10, "Ten acres of vineyard will not produce even six gallons of wine. Ten baskets of seed will yield only one basket of grain."[xiv] Leviticus 26:26, "When I destroy the source of your bread, ten women will bake bread in one oven. Then they'll return back your bread by weight. You'll eat but won't be satisfied."[xv] I could literally go but I am sure you get the point by now how God responds to those who intentionally withhold from Him what is His.

Do you know how many withhold their giving yet

stand in the presence of God and ask for His blessings? Some say, "I can't afford to give," when the truth of the matter is, we cannot afford NOT to give. Giving to the Lord's work (for He does not need money but His work does), is a test of our faith. It all boils down to the question, "Do we trust God in finances?" 1 Kings 17:7-16 recalls the story of Elijah the prophet and a starving widow. This woman and her son were dying of starvation yet Elijah approached her asking for food and even had the audacity to want to eat it first! Do you trust God to give sacrificially when you have very pressing financial matters in your home? Who takes precedence in your finance, God or Mammon? When that widow woman released her faith, (her food), the Lord opened windows from Heaven and poured over her life continually. He even raised her son back to life. Giving has the power to attract more money AND it has resurrection power. Giving is a power gift because in giving, supernatural exchanges begin. Luke 6:38, "Give, and it shall be given unto you; good measure, pressed down, and shaken together, and running over, shall men give into your bosom. For with the same measure that ye mete withal it shall be measured to you again."

People have made every excuse in the book as to why

they can't or don't give. They don't like the preacher. They have too many bills. They only have but so much. The Lord doesn't need money. The church is wasteful. They don't believe in tithes and so on, are the just some of the arguments people make as to why they don't give to the Lord. But they will flood the prayer lines and altars wondering why the Lord hasn't moved in their life yet. They wonder why they can't make ends meet. They wonder why disease is running through their bodies. They wonder why curses are active in their homes and they have most often have failed to consider that in the words given to Apostle Paul, Jesus said, "It is hard to kick against the pricks." You cannot resist the Lord and think you've won.

How should we give?

New Covenant people are regular givers. We give weekly. No one has to chase us, call us, inbox us, or put our names on a 'dead beat' list to make us give. We want to give. We give of our own worth and work. We give intentionally and purposefully. We give as God has prospered us. We give in abundance even when it is painful; sacrifice means something has died.

Our wealth as Kingdom people is not dictated by our account balances. The early church gave all to the work of ministry and they were filled with joy having no worries. Our wealth is determined by what Heaven thinks of us. We are wealthy if we can hear God for ourselves. We are wealthy if our children rise up to bless God. We are wealthy if we have plenty of possessions and I am not talking about financed ones either. We are wealthy if we have joy and can celebrate our God without fear of reprisal. We are wealthy if we worship for this is what brings God to us. We are wealthy if angels delight to be in our company. We are wealthy if we are healthy. We are wealthy if we are wise and we are wealthy if we have a sound mind. Wealth is not a dollar amount but a state of being.

Thoughts to Ponder:

Are you a tither? Explain your answer.

Share your testimony of a time when you or someone you know experienced a financial curse of the Lord.

Could God trust you as a millionaire? Explain.

7

OVERCOMING THE IDENTITY CRISIS

Despite the current title snatching wave that the corporate church is currently experiencing, the church is in a serious crisis because many saints do not know who they are. They are inundated by social media with its competitive posting, cutting edge graphics and flyers, bigger and better churches, conferences, and programs and everybody is just trying to be somebody. Folks are just trying to fit in where they can get in. It's sad really because at the end our life's journeys, we will all be asked what we have done with the time spent on the earth as humans. What will we say to the Lord when we finally make the gruesome discovery that we spent our entire sanctified life imitating someone else? Or worse, fitting a garment we were never designed to wear. Can you imagine the offense to the One who made us in His image as we try to fit into someone else's? Psalm 139:14, "I will praise thee; for I am fearfully and wonderfully made: marvellous are thy works; and that my soul knoweth right well." Genesis 1:27, "So God created man in his own image, in the image of God created he him; male and female created he them." You and I were never made as clones. We are the created kings and princes of God and we to bear forth His image. Why do we start here with identity? Because as we embark upon our destiny as people of God, of which we are all called (Matthew 22:14), we need to know who we are.

It is vitally important for every believer, ministers especially, to know who God called them to be. Jesus spent 33 years on earth as an incarnated human. He was on purpose and everything He did was purposeful which was to bring God glory. Likewise, we all have been born with set times on the earth. We are all to be good stewards of the years of life the Father has granted us. It is our responsibility to seek the Lord to find out what our vocations are and pursue them fiercely. We should let nothing and nobody deter us from the path called 'purposeful pursuit of our passion.' Romans 8:35-39, "Who shall separate us from the love of Christ? shall tribulation, or distress, or persecution, or famine, or nakedness, or peril, or sword? As it is written, For your sake we are killed all the day long; we are accounted as sheep for the slaughter. No, in all these things we are more than conquerors through him that loved us. For I am persuaded, that neither death, nor life, nor angels, nor principalities, nor powers, nor things present, nor things to come, Nor height, nor depth, nor any other creature, shall be able to separate us from the love of God, which is in Christ Jesus our Lord." This settles it. We should let NOTHING separate us from the love of God.

Identity Comes With Responsibility – Genesis 37

Jacob made a coat of many colors for Joseph. That coat was made for Joseph and him only. His brothers did not have one because Jacob didn't see qualities in them suitable for such a coat. It's not that he was better than they, but they lacked what he had. Consider this. The coat (mantle) God made for you is for you. No matter who wants it, desires it, or tries to imitate it, it is yours. No one can take away your identity in the Lord. Either a person is ignorant and don't know who they are or they allow their identity to be stolen when they are out place.

Joseph was instructed to go to Shechem to see about his brothers. They were not in Shechem, they were actually in Dothan. Jacob did not tell Joseph to go to Dothan. He only had permission from this father to travel as far as Shechem. Once he arrived in Shechem and did not see his brothers, he had a duty to report back to his father. Instead, Joseph inquired about them, decided of his own accord to pursue them, and wandered beyond his place of grace. Just because you have a mantle, assignment, calling, etc., you are still required to be responsible and accountable. Just as Joseph wandered into danger even after obeying his father, we too, by the sin of assumption, can wander out of our lanes into places of danger where the enemy lurks to compromise our garment.

Does the Father Know Who You Are?

Before Jesus was released into public ministry, the Father made a public affirmation of His identity after He was Holy Spirit filled. Matthew 3:17, "And lo a voice from heaven, saying, This is my beloved Son, in whom I am well pleased." Why was it important for the Father to affirm His identity? Because the enemy was hot on Jesus' heel to attempt to seduce him with lies about who He was. Matthew 4:3, "And when the tempter came to him, he said, If thou be the Son of God, command that these stones be made bread." Matthew 4:6, "And saith unto him, If thou be the Son of God, cast thyself down: for it is written, He shall give his angels charge concerning thee: and in their hands they shall bear thee up, lest at any time thou dash thy foot against a stone."

Warriors in Life

There had always been a question about the Lord's identity. Even His own disciples were unsure of who hH He was. Out of 12 disciples, only Peter received the revelation from the Father concerning Jesus' true identity. Matthew 16:16, "And Simon Peter answered and said, Thou art the Christ, the Son of the living God."

As soon as God confirmed Jesus' identity, the battle over who He was began. Luke 22:70, "Then said they all, Art thou then the Son of God? And he said unto them, Ye say that I am." It is essential that before you begin any work in the Lord that you have a knowing of who you are and what you are called to do because there is an adversary of your salvation who will stop at nothing until he confuses you about who you were called to be in the faith and seduces you to walk in another man's shoes. If you don't know your prophetic destiny and remain ignore the sent ones to your life who are destined to help you, the enemy can attack your life with spirits of identity theft and completely shut down who God made you and frustrate the destiny that God has placed upon your life. The life of King Saul more than validates this statement.

Holy Spirit

Thoughts to Ponder:

Have there been times in your life when you

questioned who God called you to be? Explain.

In reference to Joseph and his brothers, explain what happens when we venture beyond our place of grace.

Explain why public affirmation of a person's call is so important.

8

OVERCOMING ISSUES WITH CHURCH LEADERSHIP

Despite the throngs of people we see in leadership positions, genuine leadership is becoming more of a precious jewel. Especially in the Church, sincere and sold out men and women of God are becoming harder to find because it takes integrity not celebrities to effectively impact the Kingdom of God and sadly, many have gotten their priorities confused. 1 Samuel 13:14, "The LORD hath sought him a man after his own heart, and the LORD hath commanded him to be captain over his people". Ezekiel 22:30, "And I sought for a man among them, that should make up the hedge, and stand in the gap before me for the land, that I should not destroy it: but I found none." Not only are the people looking for Godly leadership but God is looking for His leaders. Genesis 3:9, "And the LORD God called unto Adam, and said unto him, Where art thou?"

Delisa Lindsey

The Lord is not looking for perfect people but willing people. None of us are perfect and will never be until the day of Christ so to expect flawless leadership is absurd because we all are flawed, but what we should expect is shepherds after the heart of God. Authoritative, spiritual, and sacrificial is what a leader must be in order to effectively lead the flock of the Lord. Let's look at a few character traits a Godly leader should possess.

In his book, "Spiritual Leadership", J. Oswald Sanders impeccably teaches the Body of Christ on the dynamics of spiritual leaders. I will share a few points he made.

- True greatness, true leadership, is found in in giving yourself in service to others, not in coaxing or inducing others to serve you.
- Spiritual leaders are not elected, appointed, or created by synods or church assemblies. God alone makes them.
- There is no such thing as a self-made spiritual leader. A true leader influences others spiritually only because the Spirit works in and through him to a greater degree than in those he leads.
- A leader must be calm in crisis and resilient in disappointment.

Warriors in Life

- Do you direct people or develop people?
- If you would rather pick a fight than solve a problem, do not consider leading the church. The Christian leader must be genial and gentle, not a lover of controversy.
- Many who aspire to leadership fail because they have never learned to follow.
- A visionary may see, but a leader must decide. [xvi]

John Maxwell also authors a prominent book, "The 21 Indispensable Qualities of a Leader: Becoming the Person Others Will Want to Follow", on the topic of leadership. He lists several necessary traits a leader must possess.

- Character Brings Lasting Success with People
- Commitment: It separates Doers from Dreamers
- Look at how you spend your time, are you really committed or do you just say you are?
- Simplify your Message- It's not what you say, but also how you say it
- "Competence goes beyond words. It's the leader's ability to say it, plan it, and do it in such a way that others know that you know how- and know that they want to follow you.

1/11/17

two sides to ever story

Delisa Lindsey

- Smart leaders believe only half of what they hear. Discerning leaders know which half to believe
- A leader who knows what his priorities are but lacks concentration knows what to do but never gets it done
- **Cultivate the Quality of Generosity in Your Life**
- They Know What They Want, They Push Themselves to Act, They Take More Risks, and They Make More Mistakes
- Listening: To Connect With Their Hearts, Use Your Ears
- Your People Are a Mirror of Your Attitude
- You can measure a leader by the problems he tackles. He always looks for ones his own size
- Who you are determines who you attract.[xvii]

Biblical Qualifications of Godly Leadership

"A bishop then must be blameless, the husband of one wife, temperate, sober-minded, of good behavior, hospitable, able to teach; not given to wine, not violent, not greedy for money, but gentle, not quarrelsome, not covetous; one who rules his own house well, having his children in submission with all reverence (for if a man does not know how to rule his own house, how will he be

---

Cultivate = to prepare and use (soil) for growing plants: to grow and care for = to grow or raise something under conditions that you can control (2 develop a characteristic or feature that someone/something has # *serious matters*

Quality = how good or bad something is = A characteristic or feature that someone/something has = A high level of value or excellence: for people who care about excellence

Generosity = the quality of being kind, understanding, and not selfish: the quality of being generous willingness to give money & other valuable things to others = bounty, unselfishness

able to take care of the church of God?); not a novice, lest being puffed up with pride he fall into the same condemnation as the devil. Moreover he must have a good testimony among those outside, lest he fall into reproach and the snare of the devil." (I Timothy 3:2-7)

When choosing leaders it is imperative that their lives are in line. An examination of knowledge and character should be thorough and complete. The servants of God need to be trustworthy. For anyone desiring the position of pastor or teacher, let Scripture be the guide. Keep in mind that the qualifications are clear and easier to understand than to apply.

"But let these also first be tested; then let them serve as deacons, being found blameless." (I Timothy 3:10) Pastors and leaders should be tested and tried. A good reputation and testimony really do take a lifetime to build. Knowledge of doctrine and theology coupled with integrity are the ingredients to effective leadership."[xviii]

Thoughts to Ponder:

Explain the most outrageous case of identity crisis in the Church you have ever experienced, even if means your own.

some / our leadership/leaders

Delisa Lindsey

Explain the modern day <u>challenges of leadership</u> in ministry.

- one side minded
- immaturity
- favoritism
- fake it till you make it
= luke warm at times
- Nike pick others flaws in private + public

9

OVERCOMING THE MESSINESS OF MINISTRY

Ministry is messy. Mess is an integral part of ministry because ministry has to do with people and people are messed up. Our perfect model of ministry is none other than Jesus himself and his ministry was messy. He touched lepers. He wept with grieving families. He hung out with what we might consider the lowly: children, gentiles, tax collectors, hookers, even gentiles. Ministry is, ultimately, about Jesus living in you and through you. Ministry is being his hands and feet, sacrificially serving others today as He did 2,000 years ago.

Nothing we will be called to do in service to others will be as messy as what Christ did on our behalf. He will never call us do to something for others that he hasn't done, to a far greater extent, for us. Recognizing this changes our perspective. When a person decides to take seriously the challenge to become an ambassador for Christ and to develop a mindset of ministry, he takes one of two approaches. Either he tries to learn and impart skills, or he focuses on allowing the Spirit of Christ to change his thinking and character. Only the latter approach will allow him to serve from a Christlike spirit of humility and selflessness. Yet how few seminaries concentrate on development of character even half as much as they concentrate on development of skills or knowledge? Ministry should flow out of who we are. Ministry must come out of our relationship with Christ as we respond to God's invitation to join him in what he is doing.

A true ministry mindset understands how dispensable we are, and that it's only because of God's grace that we are invited to join him in his work. Realizing that the work is his allows us to take great risks. As he calls us to step out in faith, esteeming his agenda above our own, we can respond like children jumping into the arms of a Father who has promised not to drop us, will not drop us, cannot, in fact, drop us.

This kind of adventure is truly rewarding. It's not always fun. It's certainly not convenient. But it is the only sure path to contentment and joy. To play a part in altering another person's eternal destiny…can anything compare to that kind of fulfillment? It causes a sense of enormous gratitude to well up inside our otherwise miserly hearts."[xix]

Delisa Lindsey

10

OVERCOMING WHILE LIVING WITH UNBELIEVERS

If there is anything that breaks the heart of a child of God it's trying to live with family members who aren't saved. One can hardly describe the gut tearing feeling of wanting to see salvation take place in the lives of a spouse, child, or other extended family member and see them pull away from the outstretched hand of the Lord. The duty to yet serve the Lord in spite of the stress that permeates the living environment of a believer is still required of us. It takes a Special Forces soldier to stand in the Army of the Lord when they are fighting civil war on the home-front, but many are engaged in these types of battles each and every day, silently suffering, wounded warriors still working.

Every believer wants to see their family saved and it is heartbreaking to know that hell will be their final destination if they don't receive the Lord, Jesus Christ as personal Lord and Savior. Once you pray and live this life of faith as a witness in front of them, there is nothing else you can do for a person but to place them in God's hand and leave them there. If you attempt to frighten them into the Kingdom of God or manipulate them in any way, you are only hindering their genuine salvation and are hampering any effort the Lord has made toward them on your behalf. No matter how 'slow' the Lord may be moving upon the heart of your loved ones, cease the notion to 'help Him'. The Lord has been saving people for millennia and He has done an impressive job of redeeming mankind. He does not need our help as such.

Contrary to popular opinion, satan does not have the final word about our families. Even if they are unsaved, as long as they have breath remaining, they have an opportunity for salvation through Christ as long as we continue to pray. As believers, our job is to intercede. Intercession is taken from the Latin word meaning, 'going between'. 1 Timothy 2:1, "I exhort therefore, that, first of all, supplications, prayers, intercessions, and giving of thanks, be made for all men." In the case that your loved one is a sinner, God cannot respond to their prayers but if you, the righteous one, stands in the gap for them, God will respond to you on their behalf. Psalm 66:18, "If I regard iniquity in my heart, the Lord will not hear me."

Just as Jesus becomes our advocate and He stands before the Father for us, when we intercede for others, we advocate for them. "If any man sin, we have an advocate with the Father, Jesus Christ the righteous", I John 2:1. Therefore, it does not matter how hardened a sinner your loved one may be, as long as you make up the hedge (covering/protection), the Lord will continue to bring opportunities for salvation before them. Though you stand proxy for them, the decision to choose the Lord over satan is still theirs to make. Joshua 24:15, "And if it seem evil unto you to serve the LORD, choose you this day whom ye will serve; whether the gods which your fathers served that were on the other side of the flood, or the gods of the Amorites, in whose land ye dwell: but as for me and my house, we will serve the LORD." Prayer is our obligation. Answering our prayers is God's obligation but the decision to receive salvation belongs to the individual. What helps in this area is if the person has had some prior knowledge of the Lord, been raised in the Lord, or have had some contact with another believer. Notwithstanding, the Lord can still move upon the hardest of hearts but having a template of faith to with begin certainly helps to expedite the process. In other words, when the Word of God tells us to 'train our children' (Prov. 22:6), it's not just for them to dress nice for church each Sunday. It's because if a foundation of the Word has been laid in a person's heart from a child, when the seed of the Word is released as a result of your prayers, the ground has already been tended and is more likely to receive the seed. Nevertheless, even if there is hard ground, the Word of God is like a hammer that breaks the stone in pieces. Jeremiah 23:29, "Is not my word like as a fire? saith the LORD; and like a hammer that breaketh the rock in pieces?" This is all a matter of processing. One may take more time than the other but God is able nonetheless.

Thoughts to Ponder

We all have unbelieving family members. Some may be more extended than others but what are you doing to present the Light of Christ to them?

Has there ever been a time when you 'interrupted' the plan of God's salvation for your loved one? Explain.

Do you have a testimony of the Lord saving one of your loved ones as a result of your prayers and intercession? Explain.

11

OVERCOMING AS A MINISTER

God's grace extends to us all. Psalm 100:5, "For the LORD is good; his mercy is everlasting; and his truth endureth to all generations." In each generation, the Lord chooses at least one set person to stand on behalf of the family. Now, they are not the 'God' of that family, but they are the 'called' for that generation. Whether you are that person in your family or not remains to be seen but this person will be the 'grown up' one in the faith; the more mature believer. I make this point to prove that every family has at least one 'set person' who will influence their generation. This person is the one with the primary call upon their life. They will act as the 'priest' of their family line. When this person gets in line with God, doors from Heaven are open over the family line for salvation, prosperity, health, and etc. They are the primary ones by whom the Lord will do great exploits in the earth realm. Let's consider a few Biblical examples to confirm this theory.

Delisa Lindsey

Abraham, was called out from his kindred to follow a path that had never been embarked upon by anyone before. As an apostolic people, we would call him a pioneer or trailblazer. He stepped out of the norm among the Chaldeans in pursuit of his purpose and in search for the manifestation of the perfect will of God. I think it is important to point out that the call to service was initially placed upon Abraham's life. His wife, Sarah, was a joint heir by virtue of their marital covenant and had every right to partake in everything the Lord released for Abraham. The blessings of the Lord poured out over Abraham's life for his obedience. Lot, Abraham's nephew, was a partaker of these blessings because he was connected to Abraham. God did not call Lot, but Lot followed Abraham, served him, and also partook of the grace which was upon his life. Notice, however, that once Lot stepped out of alignment with Abraham that his life shifted taking a downward turn. God's hand of mercy was yet upon him because of Abraham's prayers, but life for him was hard. Just as a fragrance which smells sweet and strong early in the day but wears off as the day progresses, so does the grace upon a person's life that is the result of a Godly –soul tie, bond, or connection that has been disconnected or dissolved.

Lot ended up in one of the worst places ever known

to man; Sodom and Gomorrah, which he thought at the time was a paradise of sort. "And Lot lifted up his eyes, and beheld all the plain of Jordan, that it was well watered every where, before the LORD destroyed Sodom and Gomorrah, even as the garden of the LORD, like the land of Egypt, as thou comest unto Zoar.", Genesis 13:10. But when he arrived and settled in, the view changed. "… Lot, vexed with the filthy conversation of the wicked." 2 Peter 2:7.

There are many other notable instances of 'heads' of families in the Bible. In Joseph's family, he was the set man. In David's family, he was the set man. In Samuel's family, he was the set man. Moses was the set man in his family although there was a tremendous call of service to Miriam and Aaron but the primary assignment went to Moses. Cornelius was the set man in his family and so on. You may or may not be the set man in your family but there is at **least** one in each family.

How do you know if you are the set one in your family? Family members will look up to you, regardless of your age or economic status. They will naturally gravitate to you for counsel, prayer, even money. If you are the set ones God has placed in your family, you have a heavy work ahead of you. Many will come to you for help but many will also scorn you, hate you, and rebel against you. Prepare yourself. Either way, your hands will be full but if God has called you as a 'father' to your generation, He has already equipped you for the battle. And if you are not the set person in your family, you still have a responsibility. Support and undergird the one who is and the Lord will tremendously bless your life. Ruth 1:16, "And Ruth said, Intreat me not to leave thee, or to return from following after thee: for whither thou goest, I will go; and where thou lodgest, I will lodge: thy people shall be my people, and thy God my God." Matthew 11:29, "Take my yoke upon you, and learn of me; for I am meek and lowly in heart: and ye shall find rest unto your souls."

Intercession for Family Members

Genesis 14:12-16, "And they took Lot, Abram's brother's son, who dwelt in Sodom, and his goods, and departed. And there came one that had escaped, and told Abram the Hebrew; for he dwelt in the plain of Mamre the Amorite, brother of Eshcol, and brother of Aner: and these were confederate with Abram. And when Abram heard that his brother was taken captive, he armed his trained servants, born in his own house, three hundred and eighteen, and pursued them unto Dan. And he divided himself against them, he and his servants, by night, and smote them, and pursued them unto Hobah, which is on the left hand of Damascus. And he brought back all the goods, and also brought again his brother Lot, and his goods, and the women also, and the people."

While Lot was in Sodom, he was robbed and taken captive. Undoubtedly, this will happen to anyone who ventures out of the will of God. John 10:10, "The thief cometh not, but for to steal, and to kill, and to destroy". The word comes to Abraham that his nephew is taken captive (bound by the enemy) and he arises to go to war to rescue him. This is the hallmark of intercession: To hear about your brother being taken captive and robbed by the enemy, to rise up in his defense to see to it that he is delivered from the hand of the enemy, and that his personal effects are returned. This is one of the best illustrations of intercession that is recorded in scripture.

In this instance, we see the power of intercession for our family members. Notice that once Abraham interceded for Lot that Lot RETURNED to Sodom! How many times have we seen this happen in our modern day? People ask for help. We pray. God delivers. And they return to the stronghold that we risked our necks to set them free from in the first place!! Gotta love family, right? 2 Peter 2:22, "But it is happened unto them according to the true proverb, The dog is turned to his own vomit again; and the sow that was washed to her wallowing in the mire."

Once again, Lot found himself in a heap of trouble. This time it wasn't a king that kidnapped him. The King of all kings was kindling His wrath against Lot's hometown. His life was in grave danger, although he didn't know it, and once again, Abraham rose to the occasion to intercede for him and his family. Genesis 18:20-23, "I will go down now, and see whether they have done altogether according to the cry of it, which is come unto me; and if not, I will know. And the men turned their faces from thence, and went toward Sodom: but Abraham stood yet before the LORD. And Abraham drew near, and said, Wilt thou also destroy the righteous with the wicked?"

Abraham, a friend of God who held the captive audience of the King of all Glory, interceded not only for Lot but for each and every believer in Sodom and Gomorrah. The Lord allowed it knowing full well that Lot was the ONLY righteous one left but He entertained Abraham's prayer just the same. (Case in point, just because we pray for a thing does not mean it will happen.

Some of our prayers have no validity and no basis for coming to pass whatsoever but God will listen to us nonetheless while He knows full well what the end result will be. I would compare it to your loving child asking for a slice of fruit and you entertain their presence out of pure love for them knowing full well that you ate it all but you won't yet tell them because it may end the pleasure of their company.) Again, God will listen to your prayer but the choice to answer remains with Him. James 4:3, "You ask for something but do not get it because you ask for it for the wrong reason—for your own pleasure."[xx]

The Lord answered Abraham's prayer. He sent angels into Sodom and Gomorrah to warn Lot and to deliver his family. Because the ways of Sodom were so engrafted into their personalities, it was a hard thing to drive them from that place but the angels succeeded nonetheless. Who can resist the power of God? They warned Lot and his family to not look back or they would be destroyed but his wife chose to sneak one last peek and it would indeed be her last. This case of intercession by Abraham on Lot's behalf is one of the most clearest ever. When there is a 'priest' in the family who can stand on the people's behalf, the Lord will extend an opportunity for salvation to the family. It will still remain the family member's sole responsibility to respond to the call for the Lord will not force them to choose but they will indeed be more privileged than those for whom there is no prayer.

12

OVERCOMING WITH UNBELIEVING SPOUSES/FAMILY MEMBERS

Living with an unbeliever is difficult for a believer but even more so challenging for ministers. The reality of living with unsaved loved ones hits even closer to home for them. For one thing, there is the burden in knowing how the Lord feels about their unsaved loved one. But there is an image many expect them to uphold that is just as tiring as the drama many have to contend with. There is pressure from the world to live the 'perfect life' although no one really knows what that means. Christian marriages are supposed to be happy, children are supposed to be compliant. Families are supposed to be supportive and then life happens.

Many times your own calling as a minister or believer are compromised and brought into question because of your living arrangements. If a minister has an unsaved or backslidden spouse, people frown. They are too noble to express their disapproval to your face but they will certainly talk about you behind closed doors. If a female minister is single or divorced, many times her integrity is called to the carpet. Again, people won't mention anything to her face but she may be discriminated against based on her social status. A pastor whose son has had trouble with the law may feel the heat of evil observers who question his authority as a pastor based on his son's misconduct. Or the first family may undergo a firestorm of criticism if found that their daughter is pregnant and unwedded. This is life. Things happen. How will you handle who God called you to be when your family is laden with problems?

What do you do when you have done all you know to do? What do you do as a minister when your spouse is unfaithful? What do you do as a minister and your children act like fools who never knew God? Do you step down? Do you walk away? Do you take on the role of Job's wife and curse God and die? What do you do? I will tell you what you do. You stand. Ephesians 6:10-17, "Finally, my brethren, be strong in the Lord, and in the power of his might. Put on the whole armour of God, that ye may be able to stand against the wiles of the devil. For we wrestle not against flesh and blood, but against principalities, against powers, against the rulers of the darkness of this world, against spiritual wickedness in high places. Wherefore take unto you the whole armour of God, that ye may be able to withstand in the evil day, and having done all, to stand. Stand therefore, having your loins girt about with truth, and having on the breastplate of righteousness; And your feet shod with the preparation of the gospel of peace; Above all, taking the shield of faith, wherewith ye shall be able to quench all the fiery darts of the wicked. And take the helmet of salvation, and the sword of the Spirit, which is the word of God"

When you have done all you know to do to present yourself as a living sacrifice to God, you stand. There is no need to buckle and run. You must still stand even all around you is falling to pieces. Granted, there will be times when you must retreat to a place where God can heal and restore you, but to throw in your towel for the sake of someone else's refusal to live right is completely unacceptable. Consider this married man who was called to do great and mighty things in the name of the Lord. His name was King David. He was a man who loved to praise and glorify God but his wife didn't share his zeal. She didn't have a heart for the Lord like he did and could have cared less about giving God a praise for anything. She kept quiet for a season and grew bitter day by day but one day she just couldn't hold her mule. She offended her husband as he was in the presence of God. He rebuked her and then God finished the sentence for him, literally. 2 Samuel 6:23, "Therefore Michal the daughter of Saul had no child unto the day of her death."

It takes someone in ministry to be married to an unbeliever to truly understand the agony that an unequally yoked marriage brings. You can't read about it and know, you have to actually live through it. The reason it is so unfair to judge a minister who is married to an unbeliever is because they face storms in life that coupled believers don't ordinarily face. Abigail was married to a fool named Nabal. He dishonored her, God, and the man of God. The result, God killed him. 1 Samuel 25:38, "And it came to pass about ten days after, that the LORD smote Nabal, that he died." What is sad is that many saved spouses give up the fight for their marriage. Unlike Abigail, many would rather cave in to their unsaved spouse's desires to pull them away from the faith than to stand as she did and let the Lord fight her battles.

Paul gives solid advice to unbalanced marriages in 1 Corinthians 7. The entire chapter is noteworthy but we will select just a passage to review. 1 Corinthians 7:15, "But if the unbelieving depart, let him depart. A brother or a sister is not under bondage in such cases: but God hath called us to peace." When a marriage has placed undue heavy strain and stress on the believer, God will allow the believer a season of peace by driving the unbeliever away. This is similar to Judas' betrayal of Jesus. When Judas departed, he entered into darkness but Jesus was ushered to another place in glory. Ruth's husband departed and she married Boaz. Abigail's husband departed and she married King David. Vashti departed and Ahaseurus married Esther. Sometimes unsaved spouses are on assignment from the enemy to hinder and in those cases, the Lord will step in and drive them away.

In other more positive cases, the Lord may allow the unsaved spouse to watch the life of the believer and if the saved spouse can live a prominent life of faith and bear a witness of the Lord Jesus to their unsaved loved one, their heart can be softened toward the word of God and becomes suitable ground to receive the word of salvation. 1 Corinthians 7:14, "For the unbelieving husband is sanctified by the wife, and the unbelieving wife is sanctified by the husband: else were your children unclean; but now are they holy." I Peter 3:1, "Likewise, ye wives, be in subjection to your own husbands; that, if any obey not the word, they also may without the word be won by the conversation of the wives."

In either case, it is through much prayer, intercession for marriage especially, that the believing spouse must carry the burden of the marriage. God knows and the final decision is His. He knows if the spouse is a 'vessel of wrath' who will refuse the voice of the Lord until the day of their death or if the spouse is a 'vessel of mercy' who will heed the word of the Lord and join the Christian band (Romans 9:22-23). Only God knows, but it is the spouse's duty to birth out the answer in prayer and to remain faithful to the Lord in the process.

Ministers with Unsaved Children

What a burden it is to love the Lord with all of your heart and then to have your children despise Him. Every normal human being wants the best for their children and every believer should want to see their children saved. Even the Father's heart aches when His children are not in the place where He desires for them to be. How heavy His heart must have been when He stood in the place where

He and Adam would commune and discovered that Adam was not there. Genesis 3:9, "And the LORD God called unto Adam, and said unto him, Where art thou?" It's not that the Lord did not know where Adam was but He wanted Adam to know that he had moved out of place. All throughout the corridors of time throughout the Old Testament the Lord called out for His children. He missed the fellowship with them and longed for their communion.

Luke 15:11-32 records the heartbreaking story of a father and his prodigal son. It tells how the son asked for his inheritance and took to the streets to squander it. The son hit rock bottom and despite the fact that he abandoned his father's home, the father had mercy on his son and kept a prayer on his heart for his son's return. Thankfully, the son returned home to his father and was safe from the cares of this life. How many can identify with the loss this father felt as his son left home? You can only imagine the feeling this father felt as he hearkened to his son's request knowing full well that the young man was ill prepared for what was to come. The father could have withheld the provisions and forced the son to stay home but he loved his son enough to allow him to make his own decision even though the consequences would be hard for him to bear.

Parents with unbelieving children have to trust the Father to see about their children when they are out of the way. A child cannot live with their parent forever and they surely cannot follow them everywhere. If they have reared their children well and their children wander astray, they have to remain confident in the God of OUR salvation that what He promised to do for them and through them will come to pass despite the child's current lifestyles. The father of the prodigal son trusted God. He stood at the door waiting for his son's return and likewise, parents of children who have gone astray, must stand in a place of expectation for their return.

God honored the prodigal's father and returned his son home to him. Because the Father has no respect of persons, He will also honor our prayers for our children if we can learn to trust Him. If we can be the example to them and parent them by the promptings of Holy Spirit, we can see the hand of God move upon our children's lives.

David had a son named Absalom who led a revolt against him. I shared early on about the rape of Tamar by her half brother Ammon. It was Absalom who rose up in Tamar's defense and murdered Ammon. Absalom never recovered from the weak use of David's authority as king because he refused to punish Ammon according to the Law. David was supposed to put Ammon to death for raping Tamar but his misjudgment caused even more wrath to be stirred within his house.

2 Samuel 15:6,13-14, "Absalom stole the hearts of the men of Israel. And there came a messenger to David, saying, The hearts of the men of Israel are after Absalom. And David said unto all his servants that were with him at Jerusalem, Arise, and let us flee; for we shall not else escape from Absalom: make speed to depart, lest he overtake us suddenly, and bring evil upon us, and smite the city with the edge of the sword."

The Lord did not intervene in this case between David and Absalom because David was in the wrong. David's sins were finding him out and he had to pay the price. In the end, Absalom was murdered by David's own generals in order to protect David's life. Sadly, because David over-loved his children and would not correct them, the Lord stepped up to the plate and punished his children. Let this be a reminder to us that though we all love our children, we should never place them above the law. They can never come before God nor stand in between us and His word. When the Father tells us to correct our children, we must do as He says.

Eli was another father who refused to correct his children. His sons were prostituting the women at the gates of the temples. These detestable acts were being reported to Eli yet he did nothing to correct his sons' illicit behavior. 1 Samuel 2:12,17, 22-25, "Now the sons of Eli were sons of Belial; they knew not the Lord. Wherefore the sin of the young men was very great before the Lord: for men abhorred the offering of the Lord. Now Eli was very old, and heard all that his sons did unto all Israel; and how they lay with the women that assembled at the door of the tabernacle of the congregation. And he said unto them, Why do ye such things? for I hear of your evil dealings by all this people. Nay, my sons; for it is no good report that I hear: ye make the Lord's people to transgress. If one man sin against another, the judge shall judge him: but if a man sin against the Lord, who shall intreat for him? Notwithstanding they hearkened not unto the voice of their father, because the Lord would slay them."

It is not a sin to love your children, but it is a grave sin to love them more than loving the righteousness of God. Eli could not differentiate the two. As the high priest, he was held to stricter standards than others. He knew better. He was a descendant of the Aaronic priesthood. He should have known that God killed priests who defiled His Temple. It is often said that preacher's kids are the worst kind. That is simply not true, it's just that preacher's kids have more exposure than others and when they commit sin their deeds are made public by virtue of their parent's position. In Eli's case, his sons were priests in the Temple. Their sins provoked the true followers of God and also negatively influenced others. Same applies to those with children in ministry. The sins of the children provoke those who are dear to the ministry, bring shame and dishonor and it also may license others to sin if they feel the sins of the preacher's kids sins are being 'lightly' addressed.

2 Samuel 4:11,16-18, "And the ark of God was taken; and the two sons of Eli, Hophni and Phinehas, were slain. And the man said unto Eli, I am he that came out of the army, and I fled to day out of the army. And he said, What is there done, my son? And the messenger answered and said, Israel is fled before the Philistines, and there hath been also a great slaughter among the people, and thy two sons also, Hophni and Phinehas, are dead, and the ark of God is taken. And it came to pass, when he made mention of the ark of God, that he fell from off the seat backward by the side of the gate, and his neck brake, and he died: for he was an old man, and heavy. And he had judged Israel

forty years."

Similar to the case of David, Eli's sons were killed. But unlike David, God also killed Eli for sparing his sons and winking at their sins. Let us understand that when our children walk contrary, as believers, ministers especially, we have Godly standards we must adhere to. We cannot compromise with them, we cannot pet them, and we cannot choose them over God. If/When our children go astray, we must tell them the truth, continue to love them, continue to pray for them, and leave them in the very capable hands of the Lord.

Thoughts to Ponder

What is the 'set person's responsibility in their family?

What counsel would you give a man who is married to a backslidden wife?

When was the last time you interceded for a loved one? Explain.

Assuming you are a parent, tell about a time when you had correct your child according to the Word of God and what the results were. If you are childless, draw your answer from someone you know who has gone through something similar.

Out of the Biblical illustrations we used today, which character can you most identify with; Abraham, Lot, Isaac, Joseph, Eli, David, Absalom, Abigail, Vashti, Ahaseurus, Esther, or Nabal? Explain.

Prayer for Unsaved Loved One

(As a courtesy, this prayer is offered to you on behalf of your unsaved loved ones. Place their names in the parenthesis and trust the Lord for their salvation.)

God is not willing that this person (name the person) perish, but that he or she comes to repentance – 2 Peter 3:9.

It is God's will that he or she (name the person) be saved and comes to a knowledge of truth – 1 Timothy 2:4.

This is the confidence that I have in Him, that if I ask anything according to His will, He hears me. And I know that if He hears me, whatever I ask, I know that I have the petitions that I have asked of Him. I ask for him or her (name the person) to be saved, to come to repentance, and to come to a knowledge of the truth that can set him or her free – 1 John 5:14,15.

If it is a relative: I believe that I and all of my household will be saved – Acts 16:31.

I realize that I am not in a battle with flesh and blood, but I am contending against demonic powers, wicked spirits in the heavenly sphere, who are trying to influence and control the person I am praying for – Ephesians 6:12. Jesus said in Luke 10:19, "I give you authority and power over all the power of the enemy" and so nothing shall in any way harm me.

Whatever I bind on earth is bound in the heavenly realm, and whatever I loose on earth is loosed in the heavenly realm – Matthew 18:18.

You may also pray this binding prayer (2 Corinthians 4:3,4):

Say, "Right now I bind the god of this world (Satan)

who has blinded their eyes to the truth of the gospel, and I loose the light of the gospel to shine on them and open their eyes. You spirit operating in the life of my loved one, blinding __(name)__ to the gospel to keep __(name)__ out of the kingdom of God, I bind you now. I belong to the Lord Jesus Christ. I carry His authority and righteousness and in His Name, I command you to desist in your maneuvers. I spoil your house according to the Word of God and I enter into it to deliver my loved one from your hands."

I pray that the eyes of their understanding would be opened to know the hope of their calling – Ephesians 1:18.

Lord, open their eyes to know You; open their understanding that they can understand the scriptures – Luke 24:31,45.

I pray for laborers to be sent into their path from the Lord of the harvest – Matthew 9:37,38.

I believe that I receive the answers to these scriptural prayers – Mark 11:24.

Lord, You watch over Your Word to perform it – Jeremiah 1:12.

Thank You that Your Word does not return to You

void, but it accomplishes what You intend for it to do – Isaiah 55:11.

I ask all this, Father God, in the holy name of Jesus. And I cover myself, my household, all my family, extended family, and all loved ones with the blood of Jesus, asking you to bless and strengthen us with your wisdom, Holy Spirit, salvation, and deliverance. Amen.[xxi]

13
OVERCOMING IN PHYSICAL HEALTH

"If any man defile the temple of God, him shall God destroy; for the temple of God is holy, which temple ye are." 1 Corinthians 3:17

These bodies are on loan to us for the amount of years the Lord has given us in the earth. We are stuck with the skin we are in until death do we part. From the cradle to the grave, we will have stretched our skin, grown out our hair, used up our organs, and worn our bones out from day to day living. These bodies must function as the Lord's body as well remain in tune with his. Our mouths must speak for him. Our eyes will see with him. Our ears will listen to him. Our legs will move for him. Our knees will bend to him. Our hands will heal for him. And our minds will comprehend him. These bodies of ours have tremendous work to do for the Lord therefore it is expedient that we tend to it, monitor it, and take care of it.

I will be the first to admit that I have been a

miserable governor of this body. I have not exercised it, fed it, or rested it properly. Because of that, this body has rebelled. It has swollen in areas it shouldn't. It causes pain at times. It causes fatigue and many times it just doesn't want to go for the Father. In fact, it acts like a stubborn mule sometimes because it has been mistreated! Our bodies, when mistreated, are like Balaam's donkey. It knows how the Lord feels about it and it drives us crazy until we 'act like we know'.

Diet. We are not talking about managing food as much as we are talking about what our bodies need. I am not a dietician but I do have common sense and I know that our bodies have requirements. We need water. We need nutrients and we need vitamins. We need fresh foods. We cannot live and sustain our bodies off of food packed in cans, cooked by microwaves, and saturated with sugar and salt. We need fresh food. We need lean meats, fish, and poultry preferably. We need fresh vegetables and fruits and we need balance in the timing of our meals.

We need to eat regularly and we need portions that correspond to our weight and height. We need breakfast, lunch, dinner, and snacks in between. As I stated, I am not a dietician so I won't prescribe a menu but I will make common sense suggestions. Now some may say, "What does this have to do with being a warrior?" A lot. In order to be effective in the Kingdom of God, you need to be whole and well. If not, your activities for the Lord may be limited by 'how well you are feeling'.

For some of us, there is a lot of work to do to retrain our bodies and make it our 'friend' again. Fortunately for many others, all that is required for them is maintenance. Their bodies already like them. If you treat your body well, it treats you well. It will bring you many delightful days but if you mistreat it, it will rebel, just like the earth rebels with hurricanes, tsunamis, and other natural disasters which causes us to spend extreme amounts of money for restoration.

Water. Your body, like earth, is made of 70% water. Your brain alone is made of 70% water which is why when the body is dehydrated, you feel pains in your head – headaches. Soda is a poor substitute for hydration because it is saturated with high fructose corn syrup. It is addictive in and of itself and has more acid than the body can dissolve. In fact, it takes 5-7 days of detox to restore the calcium that soda uses in the body. "Did you know that drinks high in phosphoric acid does a great job cleaning corroded battery terminals, remove rust from metal or toilet bowels? Soda can eat through the liner of an aluminum can and leach aluminum from the can if it sits on the shelf too long. Heavy metals in the body can lead to many neurological and other diseases.

Soft drinks steal water from the body. They work like a diuretic which takes away more water than it provides to the body. Furthermore, the high levels of sugar in soft drinks steals a considerable amount of water from the body. To replace the water stolen by soft drinks, you need to drink 8-12 glasses of water for every one glass of soft drinks that you consume!

Your body needs 8 - 10 glass of water per day. If you are drinking soft drinks you need to drink an additional 8 - 12 glass. I'll do the math--you need to drink 16 to 22 glasses of water per day to hydrate and replenish your body's water requirement.

Soft drinks never quench your thirst, nor your body's need for water. Constantly denying your body an adequate amount can lead to chronic cellular dehydration, a condition that weakens your body at the cellular level. This, in turn, can lead to a weakened immune system and a plethora of diseases.

The high amounts of sugar in soft drinks causes your pancreas to produce an abundance of insulin, which leads to a "sugar crash". Chronic elevation and depletion of sugar and insulin can lead to diabetes and other imbalance related diseases. This is particularly disruptive to growing children which can lead to life-long health problems.

Soft drinks severely interfere with digestion. Caffeine and high amounts of sugar virtually shut down the digestive process. That means your body is essentially taking in no nutrients from the food you may have just eaten, even that eaten hours earlier. Caffeine triggers a similar body emergency, with more essential minerals added to the event. Consumed with french-fries which can take weeks to digest, there is arguably nothing worse a person can put in their body.

Last, but not least, diet soft drinks contain aspartame, which has been linked to depression, insomnia, neurological disease and a plethora of other illness. The FDA has received more than 10,000 consumer complaints about aspartame, that's 80% of all complaints about food additives."[xxii] I think it is safe to say that we all need more water and less fast food.

Rest. After creating the world as we know it, the Father rested. He took an entire day to rest. He even blessed His rest, made it holy and sanctified it. Rest is very important and it is essential. In our society, everything is designed to steal our rest. There is too much television programming, stimulation from social media, music, and life in general that robs us of our rest. We stay up too late, wake up too early, and push ourselves to the limit each and every day doing the most. Again, we often mistreat our bodies and deprive it of its much needed rest.

Listen to your body. When it is tired, give it rest. Go to bed at a decent time so that if the Father wants to awaken you to speak to you, you are not too tired to obey His voice. When you go to sleep, turn off the television, the radio, and other distractions so you can sleep in peace and that your spirit is not battling against what is coming across the airwaves. Turn your phone off to keep your email and social media alerts from disturbing your sleep. And pray before your sleep so that your spirit is clean and that the Father is drawn to you in dreams.

Take vacations. I had a friend who would take 'Hobo Trips'. She would gather her family in a car, fill the tank with gas, pack the trunk with lunch baskets, they would choose a direction to go, and they would go. They would leave early after eating breakfast, drive as far as two hours away, find a place to visit in that city, make a day out of it, each lunch, and return home on that same tank of gas. A vacation does not have to be expensive but the getting away and the change of scenery can bring such a peace of mind. You can also find places in your local city to retreat to. The park, a movie, and a stroll through the neighborhood can offer a 'break' from the norm.

Exercise. Some of us hate this word and others love it. Exercise is essential and is very good for the body. Outside of keeping the body toned, it enhances the mood, pumps oxygen through the blood, and helps the body fight off sickness and disease. For the married – exercise is a good sexual stimulant and it helps to make you sleep better. Exercise does not necessarily require big, bulky equipment. Your exercise gear can consist of a pair of tennis shoes, a personal music player, and a bottle of water. Exercise also does not need to take a lot of time. Fifteen minutes twice a day is sufficient for a person with an active lifestyle.

It is the beginning of each new year that many make New Year's resolutions to join fitness centers, subscribe to Jenny Craig, and invest in workout gear that they barely use. Use what you have. Take advantage of your local recreation centers where you are more likely to meet people from your own neighborhood thus creating a social meeting which can speed time spent and be fun. If you feel the pull to exercise, start slow, pace yourself, and don't set extreme goals for yourself. Take one day at a time and don't beat up yourself when you miss a day. You want exercise to be routine and enjoyable, not a chore that you hate. With little changes, you can be on your way to enjoying the life that the Father created for you.

If you are need of healing, God is able. Through prayer and deliverance, sickness, infirmity, and disease can be removed from your life. Jesus healed many that were sick and afflicted. The key thing to keep in mind after receiving prayer and deliverance is to walk in your healing by faith and maintain your deliverance. That means that if God has delivered you from diabetes and healed you, realize that the enemy will bait you with sugary treats and snacks to lure you and that once you fall for the bait, diabetes has a legal right to enter your body again. What I have found is that people will come for prayer, God will heal them, and they will return to the same lifestyle of bad eating habits that caused the problem in the first place. When you are delivered from sickness and disease, ask the Father to reveal to you which foods to eat to build your immune system and to block those illnesses from returning.

14

OVERCOMING IN EMOTIONAL HEALTH

2 Timothy 1:7, "For God hath not given us the spirit of fear; but of power, and of love, and of a sound mind."

The key to the enemy overcoming us is to keep us bound in our minds. Most of all of our battles are fought in the mind. We tend to allow our thoughts to control us. We think people are talking about us and they don't have us to think about. We think people are mad with us and they are not. We think we are ugly, too big, too small, and worried about what people think about us and half the time people aren't paying any attention to us at all. We worry about bills 30 days before it is due. We are afraid of things that don't even matter. We are afraid of everything; what people say, what they will do, when we will die, and on and on. We will even find things to worry about and to be afraid of. We must stop giving the enemy room to torment us in our mind. 1 John 4:18, "There is no fear in love; but perfect love casteth out fear: because fear hath torment. He that feareth is not made perfect in love."

God wants you to have sound mind so that when He speaks to you, you don't have to filter His voice through the many other voices that are in your head. Can you imagine the Lord trying to speak to you and in the midst of Him speaking, the voices of fear of the past, fear of pain, fear of the future, fear of divorce, fear of failure, and fear of man are all speaking too? Now how long do you think it will take for you to silence all of those voices to try to determine what the Lord is saying? Too long. Any time a demon has access to you through doors of unhealed emotional wounds, confusion results. God is not the author of confusion.

Fears. Conquer your fears. As David stood in front of the giant, He stood with stones or rocks and he aimed for that giant's head. 1 Samuel 17:49, "And David put his hand in his bag, and took thence a stone, and slang it, and smote the Philistine in his forehead, that the stone sunk into his forehead; and he fell upon his face to the earth." Notice this, we are to 'bruise the serpent's head' with the word, or the ROCK which is Christ Jesus. Genesis 3:15, "And I will put enmity between thee and the woman, and between thy seed and her seed; it shall bruise thy head, and thou shalt bruise his heel." The curse from the Garden gave the enemy access to our heels, not our heads. Some of us have this thinking backwards. The enemy can hinder our movements if we don't stop him but he is not supposed to have access to our mental faculties. If we don't bruise his head, he will bruise ours which is why Apostle Paul told us in 2 Corinthians 10:5, "Casting down imaginations, and every high thing that exalteth itself against the knowledge of God, and bringing into captivity every thought to the obedience of Christ;".

The Worrier. Worry is defined as, "give way to anxiety or unease; allow one's mind to dwell on difficulty or troubles." [xxiii] The Bible clearly warns us against worry. Philippians 4:6, "Be careful for nothing; but in every thing by prayer and supplication with thanksgiving let your requests be made known unto God." Matthew 6:25, "Therefore I say unto you, Take no thought for your life, what ye shall eat, or what ye shall drink; nor yet for your body, what ye shall put on. Is not the life more than meat, and the body than raiment?" Matthew 6:34, "Take therefore no thought for the morrow: for the morrow shall take thought for the things of itself. Sufficient unto the day is the evil thereof." Luke 10:41, "And Jesus answered and said unto her, Martha, Martha, thou art careful and troubled about many things."

Worry is the sin of unbelief. It is the sin of distrust. Worry says, "I have to figure this thing out. I can't trust God because He moves too slow or He may not come through for me." Worry is an evil spirit that drains, wears, and stresses you out. How can you be effective for the Lord when your mind is in constant combat with its ownself? How can you hear a word from the Lord for yourself or another when your mind is literally worn out from worrying? Would you want a word from the Lord from someone who is always battling in their minds? Worrying takes sides against God's word and replaces it with fear. We stated earlier that God did not give us a spirit of fear.

Anger. Ephesians 4:26, "Be ye angry, and sin not: let not the sun go down upon your wrath". Are you mad? How do you interact with others? Is your voice elevated, strained, and nervous? What about your conduct toward 'that' person whom you said you forgave? Is there anger lacing your conversation to them or about them?

Anger is not evil in and of itself but when it lingers and when it is projected towards others for extended periods of time, your anger has taken a demonic twist. Again, anger, as an ordinary human emotion is not sin. Jesus was angry. "And Jesus went into the temple of God, and cast out all them that sold and bought in the temple, and overthrew the tables of the moneychangers, and the seats of them that sold doves," Matthew 21:12. David was angry. "And David's anger was greatly kindled against the man; and he said to Nathan, As the LORD liveth, the man that hath done this thing shall surely die," 2 Samuel 12:5. And even our Heavenly Father has been angry on many, many occasions and will continue to be angry. Psalm 7:11, "God is angry with the wicked every day."

The Father has been very angry in times past but these types of anger are the righteous form of anger that subsides once the issue has been resolved. But what about anger in cases such as Moses' and Cain's? Exodus 2:11-12, "And it came to pass in those days, when Moses was grown, that he went out unto his brethren, and looked on their burdens: and he spied an Egyptian smiting an Hebrew, one of his brethren. And he looked this way and that way, and when he saw that there was no man, he slew the Egyptian, and hid him in the sand." Genesis 4:6, "Then the LORD said to Cain, "Why are you angry, and why is your expression downcast?"[xxiv]

Un-tempered anger can cost you your life. It can cost you

your destiny. Anger, if left uncontrolled, can be destructive, vengeful, hateful, deadly, and downright demonic.

We all have exes. Someone somewhere has hurt us, left us, and betrayed us but how do we handle the bitterness of those experiences? Do we run to the Father for healing? Do we seek out Godly counsel? Do we pray? Or do we resolve it to ourselves to get even? Your Facebook newsfeed right now has someone manifesting fits of anger. They have no other outlets of release so they take to social media. Certain secular love songs are filled with anger toward a love gone wrong. I stumbled across a list of the 10 of the angriest love songs and while I have never head of them before, people are indeed listening and filling their spirits with these songs of bitterness, hatred, and rage stemming from the root of anger in an unfulfilled love relationship. "I'll Kill Her" by Soko, "Heartless" by Kanye West, 'She's So Cold" by The Rolling Stones, "Back to Black" by Amy Winehouse, "Common People" by Pulp, "Run For Your Life" by The Beatles, ">>>You" by Cee Lo Green, "You Oughta Know" by Alanis Morrisette, "I Hate Myself For Loving You" by Joan Jett and the Blackhearts, and "Bloody >>>" by Martha Wainwright.[xxv]

The jails are filled with angry people. Just take a look at any mugshot website and you will see visual manifestations of anger on people's faces that were caught on camera. The courtrooms are filled with angry people. Our communities are inundated with angry people. Your co-worker, neighbor, family member, and friend may be experiencing anger and are in need of getting it resolved. Anger was manifesting in Cain when he murdered Abel and anger is still running rampant in our society today. People all over and everywhere are angry.

Anger is a natural and normal emotion but when it is left to itself, untreated, and unresolved through prayer, forgiveness, and repentance, the enemy attracts himself to it and uses un-tempered anger as an entry way to invite with it the spirit of anger, forming a stronghold for other spirits to enter. As warriors, we must guard our spirits against anger and not allow it to control our lives. Un-tempered anger has caused many divorces, many job losses, and even death. If you are harboring anger against anyone, do yourself a favor and get rid of it. Forgive the person who harmed you, release them from your spirit, and ask the Father to grant you a new heart. Even David who was a man after God's heart could not build the Temple of the Lord because he had too much bloodshed on his hands. He was God's man of war but yet he was restricted in what he could do for the Lord because of his violence. 1 Chronicles 28:3, "But God said unto me, Thou shalt not build an house for my name, because thou hast been a man of war, and hast shed blood." When anger causes violence in your life, it will restrict you from moving forward in the things of the Lord. It forms a stronghold and will bind you from growing spiritually.

Jealousy. We cannot have everything we see. Proverbs 27:20, "The eyes of man are never satisfied."

The eye is never full of seeing and it will always show you what is better than what you have. Keep your eye single. In other words, watch what you gaze upon, Watch what you are staring at because what keeps drawing your attention can be a set up from the enemy to ensnare you in your emotions. I know a person who, from the moment someone enters a room, they stare a person up and down. They compare the other person's clothes and shoes to theirs because they have a spirit of jealousy. Jealousy is defined as, "feeling or showing envy of someone or their achievements and advantages."[xxvi] Jealousy has caused many to miss the mark in the Lord because they can't focus on themselves long enough for focusing on someone else. Jealous people compare notes. Like the witch in Snow White, they want to know if they are the 'fairest of them all.'

Jealous people have altered perceptions of themselves. The enemy has obstructed their vision that they cannot be truly happy for another person's blessings without desiring it for themselves. Jealousy causes a person to be double-minded, untrustworthy, and critical. Jealousy is sin because it prevents you from loving others. Jealousy will cause you to think a person is an enemy when in fact they are your victim. A jealous church member will be critical, judgmental, condescending, and competitive. They will cause great chaos in the Body of Christ because their low self-esteem has opened doors for the enemy to gain access to the church.

How do you overcome jealousy? Repent. Repent for not accepting the person God made you to be. Spend time in prayer as the Father performs spiritual surgery on your heart. When you realize how much jealousy has held you back you should run to your prayer altar, not the church altar, and grant the Father permission to cut your heart and remove what is hindering you. Train your spirit to pray for the people you have been jealous of. Ask the Father to bless them and when you see them, use this test to see whether you have truly been delivered from jealousy. If you can complement the person for the thing you once coveted about them without feeling 'some kind of way', you have overcome being jealous of them. If you find yourself having a hard time doing that, don't beat yourself up. Go back to the prayer altar and lay back down before the Father because apparently you moved too soon and there is still work He needs to perform in your heart.

We covered four very common emotions that plague most believers; fear, worry, anger, and jealousy. There are so many more that time won't permit us to cover but the bottom line is that God wants us to be emotionally whole. We are not perfect, far from it, but we should always remain honest in our emotions. Elijah was honest in his emotions toward the Lord. 1 Kings 19:10, "And he said, I have been very jealous for the LORD God of hosts: for the children of Israel have forsaken thy covenant, thrown down thine altars, and slain thy prophets with the sword; and I, even I only, am left; and they seek my life, to take it away." It is okay to feel some kind of way. Permit yourself to be human but realize that the Father has endowed us with His Spirit so that we may be taught each and every day to become Christ-like. We are yet human and God made us with emotions so that we are able to express ourselves but when we are dishonest about our feelings and fail to communicate them with the Father in prayer, we open ourselves to being taken advantage of by the enemy.

Genesis 4:7, "If thou doest well, shalt thou not be accepted? and if thou doest not well, sin lieth at the door. And unto thee shall be his desire, and thou shalt rule over him." The Lord was warning Cain that his emotions were about to write a check for him that he could not cash. He was headed for big trouble if he didn't get a hold of himself. Hasn't the Lord warned us about our feelings about certain things or people? He rebukes us as a loving Father should but do we take heed? Are we listening? Or do we proceed through the caution light like Cain and end up becoming a murderer?

If we continue on as if nothing needs adjusting, our untempered emotions can lead us to a place where we act out of character, bring Christ to open shame, and in some very sad cases, lead us straight to hell. It is not good to be 'in our feelings'. We are to walk by faith, not by feelings. Philippians 4:8, "Finally, brethren, whatsoever things are true, whatsoever things are honest, whatsoever things are just, whatsoever things are pure, whatsoever things are lovely, whatsoever things are of good report; if there be any virtue, and if there be any praise, think on these things."

15

WARRIORS IN LIFE

OVERCOMING LIFE'S CHALLENGES

For the first time in five years, I was led by Holy Spirit to conduct an open enrollment of our church's annual Apostolic College. As the senior instructor, I invited people from all walks of life to partake in what has been a private seminary for our ministers in training. I was barely prepared for the response. Students from all over the world enrolled and participated in this course, School of the Warriors, and studied along with us either on campus in Charlotte, NC, USA, or via live stream. The testimonies I have received were breathtaking. People's lives were not only being changed but they had received deliverance and breakthroughs in areas they had been bound in for years. The classes we held had become so intense at times that we had to stop, allow the students to gather themselves, and minister, counsel, and pray for them before we could resume class. The praise reports have tremendously blessed me which brings me to the purpose of this book.

Most of you who are reading this book are genuinely saved, Holy Spirit filled, and are in a walking relationship with the Lord. But even with that, many of us are facing insurmountable challenges that makes it very difficult at times to be consistent in our Christian character. Our minds can appear to be our worst enemy and it helps to know that we aren't the only ones. It helps to know that as the scriptures state, "that the same afflictions are accomplished in your brethren that are in the world." (1 Peter 5:9) In other words, no matter how many times the enemy may have whispered in our ears that we are the 'only ones' going through this, he is a liar. You are not the only one living with an unsaved spouse. You are not the only one with backslidden children. You are not the only minister who has been molested by a family member. You are not the only one who struggles in your giving. You are not alone. Millions of your brothers and sisters in the Faith are battling against the same spirits that you are. Isn't that a consolation that someone else understands?

After our class ended, I knew that I just couldn't shove the notes from the class into one of my many file cabinets to hold for another time. Someone else needed to know that they too can learn how to overcome life's challenges. While we can't change the hand we have been dealt in life, we can at least learn how to cope with it and ultimately overcome it.

It is my sincerest prayer that you found yourself in this book and that the scriptures I presented to you helped you to realize that your situation is not an isolated event. It has happened before, to someone, somewhere, and will most likely happen again. But at least now you are equipped. You have tools and weapons of knowledge now to be a source of strength for someone else.

We were created by Almighty God to overcome. In fact, the word declares that we are "more than a conquerer." (Romans 8:37) The Lord has confidence in each of us that we can endure whatever test and trial that has been sent our way. We can handle it, we just need to know how.

Rise up and live. Be the warrior, the 'man of war' that our Heavenly Father is. Overcome what happened to you, is happening to you, and will happen to you. Your purpose in life is to overcome each challenge you are faced with and witness to someone else that they too can prevail over what comes their way. Your life will testify on your behalf. You won't have to say much about how you endured, people will only look on you and behold the face of an overcomer.

Meet every challenge. Cry if you have to, scream if you have to, and when you have exercised your emotions, allow the Father to heal your spirit and make you whole. Don't let what happened to you destroy the destiny of God for you. You can live again. You can breathe again for you have been delivered from the chains of your past.

The Lord will give you beauty for your ashes and oil for your tears. Stay in the race and fight the good fight of faith. If you couldn't handle it, you wouldn't have it. You are stronger than you give yourself credit for and you have angels surrounding you to help usher you to your expected end. Rise up from the pain of yesterday and begin to embrace a new day. You are a warrior; a Warrior in Life. Be blessed. -pdl

Warriors in Life

Delisa Lindsey

ABOUT THE AUTHOR

Prophetess Delisa Lindsey is the Co-Founder of True Love Church of Refuge, Inc. located in Charlotte, NC along with her faithful husband, Apostle John Thomas Lindsey. Hailing from a long line of preachers, even as dated as the mid 1850's, Prophetess Lindsey, a covenant preacher, was born from both maternal and paternal families of ministers. Prophetess Lindsey has spent twenty years studying the word of God and served eleven consecutive before entering full time ministry. She has traveled extensively imparting the Kingdom mandate of preparation for the Glory of the Manifested Presence of the Lord Jesus Christ. Delisa has a unique gift for imparting prophetic understanding of times and seasons with a keen prophetic eye with powerful signs and wonders following. The Lord called her, The Big Eyed Prophet, indicating her spiritual ability to see into the spiritual realm and discern evil forces at work.

Prophetess Lindsey has a strong global ministry where she impacts thousands of lives almost daily as she releases fresh words of wisdom, revelation, warning, and instruction to the Body of Christ at large. Although Prophetess Lindsey is commissioned by the Lord, Jesus Christ as an Apostle, she yet remains a passionate teacher in the prophetic ministry.

Prophetess Lindsey is humbly submitted to the apostolic fathering and leadership of 'The General of Deliverance", Apostle Ivory L. Hopkins, Pilgrims Ministry of Deliverance, Harbeson, DE. She is the Senior Instructor at True Love Apostolic College, a prolific writer of bible studies, commentaries, prophetic articles, publisher, playwright, and prophetic song writer.

To order books, CDs and DVDs by Prophetess Delisa Lindsey or to help financially support her ministry, please visit: www.pdlministries.weebly.com

Prophetess Lindsey teaches and publishes each of her workbooks on the prophetic, namely, Engaging the Authentic Voice of the Prophetic, The Six Obligations of the Prophet in Spiritual Warfare, and Prophetic Keys and Prayers. Coming to print is "Developing the Prophetic Eye". All books are available for purchase at www.pdlministries.weebly.com .

Digital versions are available via Nook or Kindle and all international orders can be processed through Amazon.com.

Prophetess Lindsey, former public schools educator, has over six years of experience in teaching the School of Prophets, School of Deliverance, School of Ministry, and the School of Five Fold Ministry. She is also a prolific Old Testament studies Teacher. Many of her lessons have been recorded and are available for your private instruction by visiting www.pdlministries.weebly.com

If you are interested in hosting a School of Prophets, Advanced Training Workshop, Book Signing, or other program with Prophetess Lindsey, please contact True Love Church of Refuge by phone (980) 522-8096, email admin@truelovechurchofrefuge.org or by postal mail: True Love Church of Refuge, 5201- D Nations Ford Road, Charlotte, NC 28217 for prayerful consideration.

Delisa Lindsey

The SEX Obligations of the Prophet In spiritual WARFARE
Prophet Delisa Lindsey

Demonic
Delisa Lindsey

The Burden of Prophetic Ministry
Delisa Lindsey

BIBLIOGRAPHY

[i] http://acestoohigh.com/2012/03/13/ex-pastor-marries-science-bible-studies-to-heal-wounds-of-childhood-trauma/

[ii] http://hebrewbible.wordpress.com/2011/03/13/the-battle-of-brothers-the-old-testament-and-sibling-rivalry/

[iii] http://hebrewbible.wordpress.com/2011/03/13/the-battle-of-brothers-the-old-testament-and-sibling-rivalry/

[iv] http://www.gotquestions.org/honor-abusive-parent.html

[v] http://www.cbn.com/spirituallife/CBNTeachingSheets/keys-Overcoming_Child_Abuse.aspx?option=print

[vi] http://www.biblestudytools.com/lexicons/hebrew/nas/shamem.html

[vii] http://www.womeninthebible.net/Tamar-Daughter-of-David.htm

[viii] http://www.blueletterbible.org/lang/lexicon/lexicon.cfm?Strongs=G3126

[ix] http://www.bible.ca/ef/expository-john-1-45-46.htm

[x] http://content.time.com/time/business/article/0,8599,2048696,00.html

[xi] http://sleepfoundation.org/how-sleep-works/how-much-sleep-do-we-really-need

[xii] http://www.htmlbible.com/kjv30/henry/H12C004.htm

[xiii] Scripture quotations are taken from the Holy Bible, New

Living Translation, copyright ©1996, 2004, 2007. Used by permission of Tyndale House Publishers, Inc., Carol Stream, Illinois 60188. All Rights Reserved.

[xiv] Ibid.

[xv] The Holy Bible: International Standard Version® Release 2.1 Copyright © 1996-2012 The ISV Foundation ALL RIGHTS RESERVED INTERNATIONALLY.

[xvi] http://www.ministrygrid.com/blog/-/blogs/40-quotes-from-spiritual-leadership-by-j-oswald-sanders-part-1-

[xvii] http://www.sermoncentral.com/articleb.asp?article=John-Maxwell-94-Leadership-Quotes

[xviii] http://www.sharefaith.com/guide/books-of-the-bible/Timothy,%20the%20Son%20and%20the%20Servant/1-timothy-qualifications-of-ministry-leaders.html

[xix] https://bible.org/seriespage/leader-qualifications

[xx] The Holy Bible: International Standard Version® Release 2.1 Copyright © 1996-2012 The ISV Foundation ALL RIGHTS RESERVED INTERNATIONALLY.

[xxi] http://heavenawaits.wordpress.com/prayer-for-unsaved-loved-ones/

[xxii] http://www.getfrank.co.nz/health-fitness/nutrition/soda-soft-drinks-do-not-hydrate-your-body

[xxiii] http://www.jibaros.com/worry.htm

[xxiv] NET Bible copyright © 1996-2006 by Biblical Studies Press, L.L.C. http://netbible.com. Used by permission. All rights reserved.

[xxv] http://hellogiggles.com/top-10-angriest-love-songs

Delisa Lindsey

xxvi

http://www.oxforddictionaries.com/us/definition/american_english/jealous